TRUE TALES AND AMAZING LEGENDS OF THE OLD WEST

General George Armstrong Custer. This photo was taken two months before the Battle of the Little Bighorn. Custer posed for over 150 photographs in his lifetime.

TRUE TALES AND AMAZING LEGENDS OF THE OLD WEST

from *True West* Magazine

THE EDITORS OF
TRUE WEST MAGAZINE

Clarkson Potter/Publishers
New York

ILLUSTRATION CREDITS

Abbreviations: a, Above; b, Below; l, Left; r, Right; t, Top; m, Middle; al, Above Left; ar, Above Right; bl, Below Left; br, Below Right; tl, Time Line; BBB, Bob Boze Bell art/photo; DL, Denver Public Library; CLD, Chet and Lindy Downs, Dos Amigos Publishing Co., Jourdanton, TX 78026; PG, Phyllis Gendreau; HS, Historical Society; LC, Library of Congress; RGM, Robert G. McCubbin collection; NA, National Archives; KAR, Karen A. Robertson photo; TX, Texas State Library & Archives Commission; TW, True West archives; GW, Gus Walker map.

2 RGM; 6 Craig Fouts; 8 RGM; 10 BBB; 13 TW; 14 t GW, bl & br KAR; 15-16 KAR; 18 Charles Deas; 19 tl TW; 20-22 TW; 23 t Alfred Jacob Miller, tl TW; 24 GW; 26 Montana HS; 27 & 29 TW; 30 Henry McArdle; 31-32 TW; 34 Daughters of Republic of Texas Library; 36 BBB; 37 David Zucker; 38 Paul Hutton; 39 Center for American History U Texas at Austin; 40 TW; 42 t TX, tl TW; 43 tl TW; 45 BBB; 46 & 48 TW; 49 BBB; 50-51 RGM; 52 BBB; 53 l BBB, r RGM; 54 & 56 RGM; 57 Anthony Garnett; 58 TW; 59 NA; 60 LC; 61 RGM; 63 TW; 64 l KAR, r Idaho HS; 67 Idaho HS; 69 l RGM, r Craig Fouts; 70 TW; 73 BBB; 76 TW; 77 Craig Fouts; 78 BBB; 80 *San Francisco Call* (Dec. 15, 1896); 82-83 BBB; 84 RGM; 85-86 TW; 87 RGM; 88 TW; 90 RGM; 91 BBB; 92 & 94 TW; 97 Museum of New Mexico (Neg. No. 11409); 98 Minnesota HS; 99-100, 102 & 104 TW; 105-109 TW; 110 Dept. of Special Collections, Chester Fritz Library, U North Dakota; 111 TW; 112 TX; 113-114 NA; 115 TX; 117 NA; 119 Colorado HS; 120 t Colorado HS, tl TW; 121 t Denver HS, m DL, tl TW; 122 t & m DL, tl TW; 123 TW; 124 GW; 125 DL; 126-130 TW; 132 GW; 133 CLD; 134 t CLD, tl TW; 135 TW; 136-137 TW; 138 t CLD, tl TW; 139 TW; 140 t CLD, tl TW; 141 CLD, inset BBB; 142-143 TW; 144 CLD; 145 TW; 146 GW; 147-148 TW; 151 TW; 152 GW; 153-154 TW; 155-159 Jim Gatchell Memorial Museum; 160 & 162-164 Arizona HS; 165 RGM; 166-167 TW; 169 & 171 a Gary S. McClelland; 171 b Tombstone Western Heritage Museum; 174 BBB; 175 101 Ranch; 177 North Fort Worth HS; 178-179 101 Ranch; 180 TW; 181 PG; 182 t PG, tl TW; 183 TW; 185-186 & 188-190 PG.

Published in the United States by Clarkson Potter/Publishers,
an imprint of the Crown Publishing Group, a division of Random House, Inc., New York.

www.crownpublishing.com
www.clarksonpotter.com

All of the stories in this collection have previously appeared in *True West* magazine.

Library of Congress Cataloging-in-Publication Data

True tales and amazing legends of the Old West : from the pages of True West magazine—1st ed.
1. West (U.S.)—History—Anecdotes. 2. West (U.S.)—Biography—Anecdotes. 3. West (U.S.) —Folklore.
4. Tales —West (U.S.) 5. Legends—West (U.S.). I. True West.

F591.T695 2005

978—dc22 2005048704

ISBN 0-307-23638-2

Printed in China

Design by True West Publishing, Inc.

11 10

First Edition

ACKNOWLEDGMENTS

FOR OVER A HALF CENTURY, Old West historians have made *True West* magazine a respected source on the history of Western North America. Writers such as Glenn Shirley and Eve Ball from the magazine's early days have entertained past generations of readers by separating fact from myth, just as Joseph Rosa, Neil Carmony and other contemporary writers do now.

The editors of *True West* magazine acknowledge a debt to the historians of yesterday and today, for it is their scholarship that makes *True West* the leading authority on the history of the Old West.

Without our writers, *True West* magazine would not exist. And to them, the editors of *True West* are particularly grateful. Special thanks go to the authors who allowed us to republish their articles in this book. Choosing what to include from the wealth of articles that have appeared in the magazine was a daunting task.

The editors also wish to thank Bart Bull, who first envisioned this book, and our agent James Fitzgerald, who sold the concept to the Crown Publishing Group. For patience and perseverance in enduring our seemingly endless e-mails and for shepherding the book through the Crown production process, we thank our Crown editors Natalie Kaire and Maria Gagliano.

Finally, we thank *True West*'s art director, Daniel Harshberger, for his splendid layouts and Robert Ray, head of *True West*'s production department, for working weekends so we could meet our deadline.

—The Editors, *True West* magazine

Bat Masterson (left) and Wyatt Earp.

CONTENTS

The only known photograph of Billy the Kid.

INTRODUCTION

BY THE TIME *TRUE WEST* MAGAZINE DEBUTED IN 1953, millions of words had already been written about the wild and wooly West—most of them wrong.

Lewis and Clark's great exploration to the Pacific Ocean was already 150 years old; the goldfields that had incited a reckless dash to Colorado and Arizona and California were already played out; the billions of acres west of the Mississippi—once the domain of dozens of Indian tribes—were now officially "closed" as available land to white settlers; and a whole bevy of gunslingers and hard-drinking women were left to the imagination.

It started with the dime novels of the mid-1800s when exaggeration and fabrication became art forms. Early "biographers" of Western icons focused on larger-than-life tales, acting more like press agents than historians. From the first Western movie in 1903 to today, artistic license and sexy legend has usually been more important than historical accuracy.

But Joe "Hosstail" Small believed—and bet his new family's nest egg—that there was a market for stories that told the true story of the West—warts and all. Starting in the bedroom of their Austin, Texas, home when Dwight Eisenhower was president, Joe and Elizabeth Small created a magazine that is still leaving its mark on history.

Joe was always most pleased with the praise from one of the leading historians of his day, Walter Prescott Webb, who said: "*True West* is bringing more Old West history to life than all the rest of the press combined, including all of the history books."

He counted as a friend and fan Country singer Johnny Cash, whose career was blooming in the early 1960s when he returned the affection with the album *Ballads of the True West*.

There have been eight owners since the Smalls and all have shared the vision—today's CEO and Executive Editor Bob Boze Bell became an Old West devotee from reading *True West* magazine as a boy.

The magazine has moved from Texas to Wisconsin to Oklahoma to Arizona, but over all these years, its aim has been the same: Discovering the men and women who settled the American West; exploring their triumphs and tragedies; exposing their vices and virtues.

"*True West* isn't just a state of mind or a piece of history, but a direction," Bell says today. "It points us to who we are as Americans."

The 26 stories in these pages are a sampling of what you find when you take an honest look at the Old West. Some stories are touching, some are funny, some are disgusting. But all of them are part of the great human drama of settling the West.

As "Hosstail" Small stated in his inaugural issue, "Howdy, Pard! Sure, let's go West . . . but let's go *True West*."

SACAGAWEA'S IMPROBABLE REUNION

AN AMERICAN ICON POINTS THE WAY FOR LEWIS AND CLARK

LEWIS *and Clark didn't name a single landmark to commemorate their teenage interpreter, Sacagawea. They did honor her with "Bird Woman River," apparently thinking the white translation of her difficult name—spelled many ways, both in their journals and today—would be memorable when her native name wasn't.*

THEY WOULD NO DOUBT be astonished to discover today that her real name is as famous as theirs, and adorns scores of items, including parks and a massive lake that covers the land of the friendly tribes who helped the explorers survive a nasty North Dakota winter. Novels about her—some making incredible claims—outsell books about the expedition itself.

In real life, Sacagawea didn't fare any better when it came to a payday. Her French-Canadian husband, Toussaint Charbonneau—who cinched his interpreter job because she knew her native Shoshoni language—was paid $500.33. She received not a penny. At least Clark apologized for this slight in a letter to Charbonneau on August 20, 1806—well, sort of: "Your woman who accompanied you that long, dangerous and fatiguing rout to the Pacific Ocean and back deserved a greater reward for her attention and services on that rout than we had in power to give her." Wouldn't he be shocked today to see her face on a dollar coin, officially issued by the United States of America?

To Lewis, she was little more than "the Indian woman" who came with Charbonneau, although he did help birth her son. Clark saw more, calling her "Janey," acknowledging her contributions to the trip and eventually educating her son in St. Louis. (An affair between Clark and Sacagawea is probably myth, although the idea of one made it into a bestseller.)

Neither Lewis nor Clark realized one of the enduring legacies of their Voyage of Discovery was to make this teenager one of the most famous women in America. They would never have guessed more statues would be erected to her than any other woman of any color. Nor could they have guessed they'd given her a special status when they made her the first American woman having the right to vote. (OK, so it was only once and just on where to locate a winter fort, but her sisters wouldn't get the privilege for another century, so it's worth noting.)

Folklore and movies have made her out to be more than she was. She wasn't "*the* guide" of the expedition, as some have claimed—most of the landscape she saw was as new to her as it was to Lewis and Clark—but she did help when it really mattered, in the mountains of Montana and Idaho when she came into the Shoshoni land of her birth.

It was there that one of the unadulterated joys of the entire expedition was experienced—one glorious moment in a thousand days of hardship. It is such an incredible moment that historian and filmmaker Dayton Duncan calls it, "coincidence that would strain credulity in a fictional account."

By late July 1805, the Corps of Discovery had surmounted the Great Falls of the Missouri (near Great Falls, Montana), and reached the Three Forks, where the party rested for two days. Although Sacagawea showed no outward emotion—as far as Lewis could discern—the campsite must have brought back a flood of memories. Five years earlier, she and her native family had camped at the same spot when they were attacked by Hidatsas. The Shoshonis had fled to a nearby forest, but the Hidatsas followed, killing most of the band and taking Sacagawea, a few other women and four boys captive. They were brought back to the Hidatsa village in North Dakota, where Charbonneau won Sacagawea in a wager.

From the Three Forks, the Corps ascended the Jefferson River—which Lewis named for the president—then headed up its main Western tributary, the Beaverhead, which the two captains called a "fork of the Jefferson." While the enlisted men dragged their canoes through the rocky shallows, Lewis went ahead with a small scouting party, searching for Shoshonis. He found no one.

With autumn approaching, Lewis and Clark urgently needed to obtain horses from the Shoshonis so the Corps could pack its supplies over the Continental Divide before winter snows closed the passes.

They were counting on a convoluted interpretive dance to understand this new tribe: Sacagawea knew the Shoshoni language and also some Hidatsa, which she'd relate to her husband, who could translate from Hidatsa into French for the official interpreter, George Drouillard, who would convert it into English.

On August 8 as the expedition stopped for the evening, Sacagawea excitedly pointed at a nearby hill, calling it the "Beaver's Head" (in Montana's Beaverhead Rock State Park, north of Dillon). She remembered the formation from her childhood. Through the translations of Charbonneau and Drouillard, she informed Lewis and Clark that her people spent their summers in a valley to the west. Motioning toward the distant Beaverhead Mountains, she told the captains about a pass the Shoshonis used when going to hunt buffalo. She was positive her band would be found on the other side.

Desperate to locate the Shoshonis or some other tribe with horses, Lewis picked three men and the next morning headed toward the Continental Divide. Clark remained with the main party and their canoes, intending to continue up the Beaverhead until Lewis returned. Despite venturing into the country where Sacagawea had been raised, Lewis—for some unfathomable reason—left the young woman behind.

On August 11, Lewis and his scouts spotted an Indian on horseback, but he refused their advances and rode away. The next day, Lewis and his men crested the Continental Divide at Lemhi Pass and entered what is now Idaho. That afternoon, they drank from a creek whose waters would eventually flow to the Pacific Ocean, marking the first time the Corps of Discovery had ventured beyond the Louisiana Purchase.

On August 13, Lewis and his party descended a prominent Indian trail that led to the Lemhi Valley, west of the Beaverheads. Although the Americans spotted several Indians, the natives ran away when Lewis approached. Frustrated at being unable to make contact, he and his men headed north along the Lemhi River, and soon surprised three more Indians. A teenage girl fled, but the other two—a 12-year-old girl and an elderly woman—sat passively on the ground, their eyes downcast, no doubt certain that they were about to be killed.

Drouillard used sign language to relay the Americans' peaceful intentions, asking the Indians to recall the teenager who had run away. Meanwhile, Lewis gave the Indians a few trinkets. Losing her fear, the elderly woman signaled the teenager, who soon returned. Drouillard then coaxed the women into leading the Americans to their camp.

After covering about two miles, they encountered 60 warriors galloping to the women's rescue. When the Indians spotted Lewis and his men, they reined in their horses and eyed the Americans warily.

Knowing that a careless move could cost his party its scalps, Lewis put down his rifle and unfurled an American flag. Then in company with the old woman, he walked toward the

13 THINGS WE KNOW FOR SURE ABOUT SACAGAWEA

- Nov. 11, 1804: Sacagawea enters Fort Mandan with her husband. She's six months pregnant with her first child.
- Feb. 11, 1805: With the help of Meriwether Lewis, who feeds her a physic made of rattlesnake rattle, she gives birth to a son and names him Jean Baptiste. (Clark calls him "Pomp.")
- April 13: She calmly rescues scientific instruments and valuables being washed overboard when a pirogue almost capsizes.
- May 20: Lewis and Clark name "Bird Woman River" in her honor.
- June 10: She hovers near death alongside the Great Falls of the Missouri. She is bled repeatedly by Clark and finally recovers by drinking mineral water from a sulfur spring.
- June 29: She, Charbonneau, Pomp and Clark nearly drown in a flash flood.
- July 28: At the Three Forks of the Missouri, she calmly recounts the story of her capture by Hidatsa raiders five years earlier.
- Aug. 27: She is reunited with her brother, chief of the Shoshoni.
- Oct. 13: Her presence convinces local tribes that the expedition comes in peace.
- Nov. 24: She is allowed to vote with the men on the location of Fort Clatsop on the Oregon Coast.
- Jan. 6, 1806: Sacagawea insists on being taken to the Pacific Ocean to see a beached whale.
- July 6: She points out Bozeman Pass to Clark's party on their return trip through Montana.
- Aug. 17: She and Charbonneau remain at the lower Hidatsa village as the expedition makes its way to St. Louis and the end of its journey.

TWO IMPORTANT THINGS WE DON'T KNOW ABOUT SACAGAWEA

1. How to spell her name. Most people know her as Sacajawea (SACK'-a-ja-wee-a). In North Dakota, they insist on spelling it Sakakawea (Sa-CA'-ca-wee-a). But scholars, historians and the U.S. Geographical Names Board call her Sacagawea (Sa-CA'-ga-wee-a).
2. When and where she died. Most historians believe she died December 20, 1812, at Fort Manuel in South Dakota when she was 25. While the North Dakota Interpretive Center cites this date and place, it also adds that some historians think she renamed herself "Porivo" and lived into her nineties, dying in Wyoming in 1884.

Meriwether Lewis (top) and William Clark.

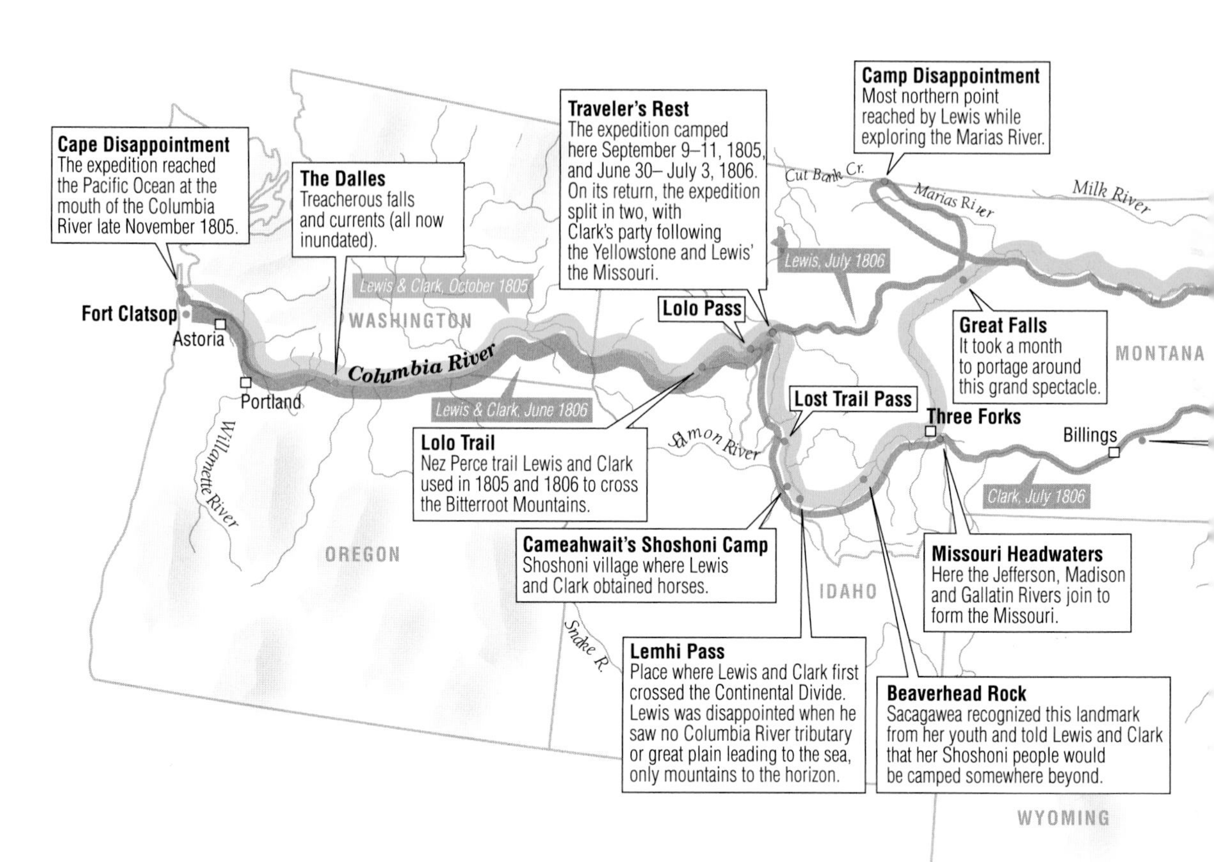

This replica of Fort Clatsop, where the Corps of Discovery spent a wet winter (1805–06), is located about seven miles from Astoria, Oregon.

The Great Falls of the Missouri—for which Great Falls, Montana, is named—required a month of backbreaking portages to surmount.

Meriwether Lewis William Clark and the Corps of Discovery

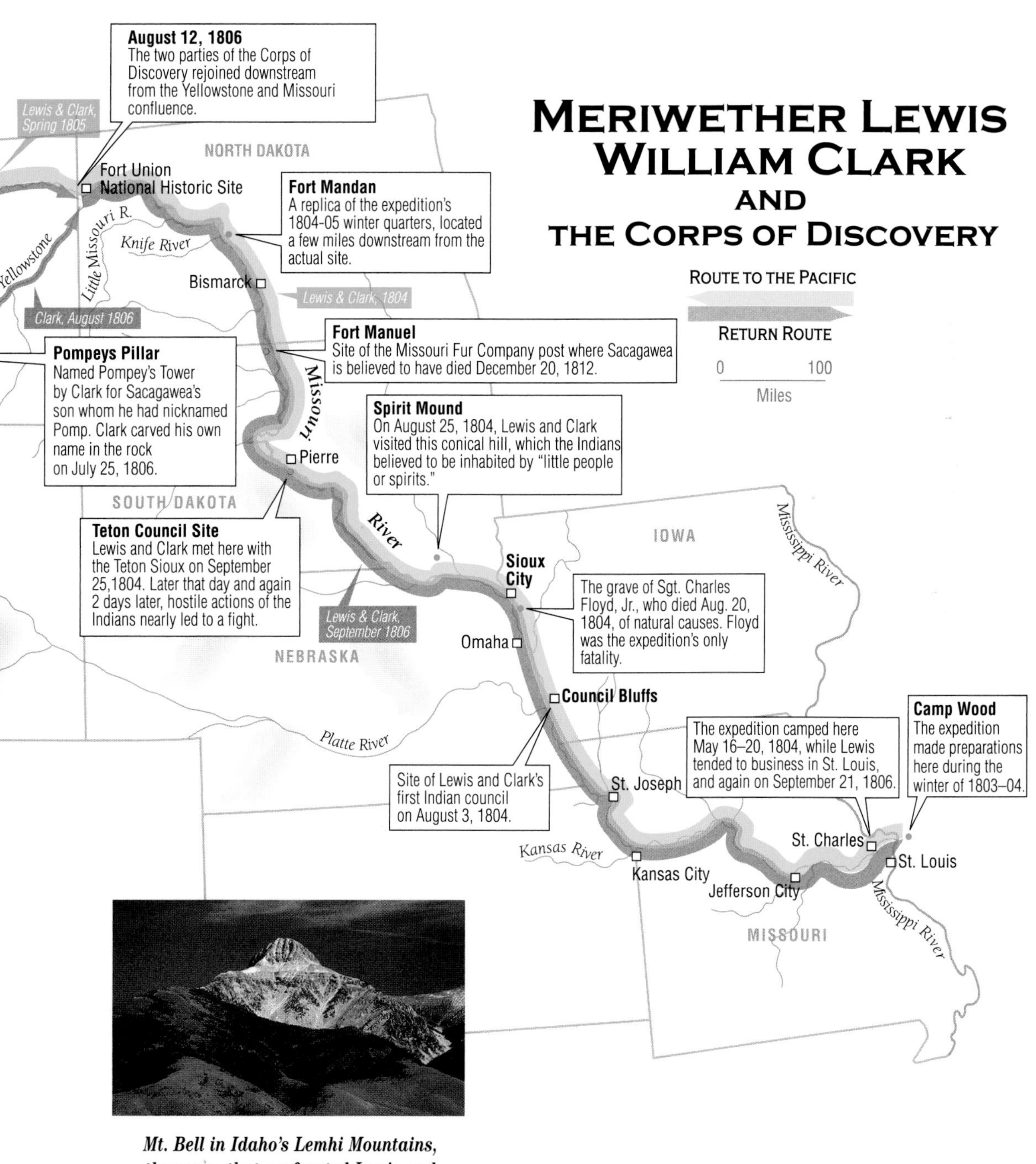

Mt. Bell in Idaho's Lemhi Mountains, the range that confronted Lewis and Clark when they crested the Continental Divide at Lemhi Pass.

Looking west after he summited Lemhi Pass, all Lewis saw were mountains. That day, the hope of a Northwest water passage died.

warriors. The woman told the Shoshonis' leader, Chief Cameahwait, that she and her two companions were unharmed and that Lewis had given them presents. The chief immediately put aside his suspicions and invited the Americans to his camp (located about seven miles north of Tendoy, Idaho).

Over the next couple of days, Lewis persuaded Chief Cameahwait and a number of his band to accompany him back over Lemhi Pass so they could rendezvous with Clark and the rest of the expedition at a place Lewis called "the forks of the Jefferson River" (now beneath Montana's Clark Canyon Reservoir). He added that the Americans needed the Indians' horses to pack their equipment over the mountains. Although the Shoshonis expressed concern about being led into a trap, Lewis promised to give them presents, saying they were with the main party. The lure of the American's gifts convinced the Indians to risk going.

On August 16, Lewis, Cameahwait and their combined entourage arrived at the place Lewis had said they would find the expedition, but Clark and the rest of the Corps were nowhere to be seen. Many of the Indians wanted to return home, fearful Lewis was conspiring with their enemies in order to massacre them. But before the Shoshonis could reach a consensus to leave, Lewis told them the Americans had with them a young Shoshoni woman who had been captured by the Hidatsas several years earlier. If they departed now, he said, they would not only miss seeing her but also a man with black skin and short curly hair—William Clark's slave, York. Their curiosity aroused, the Shoshonis decided to stay.

The following morning while Drouillard and a Shoshoni warrior headed downstream to search for the main expedition, Clark, Charbonneau and Sacagawea left their camp and walked up the Beaverhead River, looking for Lewis. Suddenly, Sacagawea began to dance and suck her fingers as she pointed at Drouillard and his Shoshoni companion.

Much to everyone's relief, the parties reunited a short time later. In the midst of much embracing, Jumping Fish, a young Shoshoni woman who had accompanied Cameahwait, recognized Sacagawea as her childhood friend. During the Hidatsa attack, she had been captured with Sacagawea, but Jumping Fish had leapt through a stream—hence her name—and escaped.

While the two women renewed their friendship, Lewis and Clark began to parley with Chief Cameahwait beneath a canvas canoe sail that had been erected as a sunshade. After smoking a ceremonial pipe, the captains sent for Charbonneau and his wife. Sacagawea was to translate Cameahwait's Shoshoni to Hidatsa, for Charbonneau to relate in French to Private Francis Labiche (he was standing in for Drouillard), who would render Cameahwait's words in English to Lewis and Clark—or so the captains hoped.

As the circuitous translation began, Sacagawea gazed intently at the Shoshoni chief as if he reminded her of someone from her past. All at once she jumped to her feet, rushed to his side, threw her arms around him and started sobbing. It took several moments for Lewis and Clark to understand why she was so distraught, but when they did, they certainly counted their blessings. Cameahwait was Sacagawea's brother.

Over the next three days, Clark, Sacagawea, Charbonneau and 11 other members of the expedition accompanied the Shoshonis over Lemhi Pass to their camp in the Lemhi Valley. Taking a native guide, Clark then headed down the Lemhi River to the Salmon—which he named Lewis' River—to see if it could be safely descended in dugout canoes. He and Lewis were hoping to discover a water route to the Oregon Coast. Clark was soon disappointed. A few miles west of present-day North Fork, Idaho, he saw enough rapids to convince him the Salmon could not be run. To do so would be suicide. It was a "river of no return."

While Clark was making his reconnaissance, back at the Shoshonis' camp, Sacagawea encountered a warrior to whom she had been promised in marriage before her capture by the Hidatsas. The ticklish situation was resolved when the warrior renounced his claim because Sacagawea had given birth to Charbonneau's son.

On August 22, Sacagawea, Charbonneau and 50 mounted Shoshonis returned to the expedition's main camp east of the Beaverhead Mountains. After caching their canoes and excess stores, the Americans packed their remaining baggage on the Indians' ponies and headed over the Continental Divide to meet up with Clark.

As August drew to a close, Lewis and Clark traded with the Shoshonis, obtaining the horses they needed for the next leg of their exploration. One can only guess about the emotional turmoil Sacagawea must have gone through as she weighed whether to remain with her people or continue to the Oregon Coast with the Corps of Discovery. In the end, the pull of adventure won out over family.

When Lewis and Clark rode away from the Shoshonis' camp, Sacagawea went with them, eventually securing her rightful place as an American heroine.

RENDEZVOUS

THE RISE OF THE MOUNTAIN MEN

BEFORE *the Oregon Trail, before the cattle drives,*

before Wild Bill Hickok and Wyatt Earp—

fur trappers and mountain men opened the West.

IN THEIR HEYDAY they numbered but a few hundred, yet these intrepid frontiersmen penetrated a land known only to the Indians and within 20 years paved the way for all who would follow.

The economic engine that drew men such as Jedediah Smith and Jim Clyman was the beaver, with its fine, barbed underhair that hatters pressed into felt and then molded into hats. Beaver pelts—"furry bank notes" as they were sometimes called—could make a man rich. All he had to do was journey into the unknown, freeze his legs in icy streams while setting his traps and risk losing his scalp to Indians or grizzly bears.

The vanguard of the mountain man era included many members of Ashley & Henry, the fur trapping partnership of William Ashley and Andrew Henry, which was a forerunner of the famous Rocky Mountain Fur Company. Some, like Clyman, were seasoned trappers; many others were simply out-of-work youngsters who entered the business by answering newspaper ads seeking "enterprizing young men" to ascend the Missouri River. Amazingly, the ads attracted many who'd leave their marks in the annals of the fur trade: Tom Fitzpatrick, Jim Bridger, Bill Sublette and the crème de la crème, Jedediah Smith, who would become not only one of the most famous mountain men but also one of America's foremost explorers.

During his first year on the upper Missouri in 1822, Smith showed his mettle and it probably surprised no one when Ashley chose him as partisan (commander) of his own trapping brigade.

In 1823, the Arikaras closed the Missouri to river traffic, which compelled Ashley to send his brigades overland from Fort Kiowa, a trading post belonging to Berthold, Chouteau & Pratte (a.k.a. the French Company) that was located about 25 miles above the mouth of the White River (near Chamberlain, South Dakota).

In late September, Smith's 12-man brigade headed west, following the White. The men walked, since their horses were needed to pack their supplies. Leaving the White, they crossed to the southern edge of the Black Hills, and then dropped into the Powder River basin. Hoping to winter among the Crow Indians, Smith dispatched Edward Rose, a seasoned trapper of mixed parentage, to find their camp.

Five days later, the brigade was moving single file through a brushy bottom when it surprised a giant grizzly, which attacked Smith, nearly ripping off his scalp. Before the other

BUILDING THE AMERICAN WEST

March 26, 1821
Hudson's Bay Company and North West Company merge under the Hudson's Bay name.

Beaver on the Missouri.

Spring–Summer 1821
William Becknell leads a freight convoy from Franklin, Missouri, to Santa Fe, New Mexico, opening the Santa Fe Trail.

August 10, 1821
Missouri enters the Union as the nation's 24th state. Jacob Hawken makes quality rifles at his 214 North Main Street armory in St. Louis.

1822
Congress abolishes the federal monopoly Indian factory trading system. John Jacob Astor reorganizes the American Fur Company, dividing it into the Western and Northern Departments.

March 9, 1822
Charles Graham receives the first patent for false teeth.

January 3, 1823
Mexico allows Anglos to colonize Texas, provided they are Roman Catholic.

August 10, 1823
Colonel Henry Leavenworth orders his Missouri Legion to shell the Arikaras in reprisal for a recent attack on American trappers.

December 2, 1823
President James Monroe publicly proposes his Monroe Doctrine.

President Monroe.

1825
John Stevens operates America's first experimental steam locomotive. St. Louis gunsmiths Jacob and Samuel Hawken form a partnership to manufacture quality rifles.

March 19, 1825
Hudson's Bay Company's managing governor, George Simpson, dedicates the firm's Fort Vancouver at Belle Vue Point on the north side of the Columbia River (across from Portland, Oregon).

Once ranging across much of the American West, grizzly bears were a formidable foe for Indians and mountain men alike.* A Tight Fix, *Arthur F. Tait (right) and* The Great American Hunter & Trapper, *S.E. Hollister (left).

trappers could kill the bear, it disappeared into the brush. Using a needle and thread, Clyman stitched the partisan back together (see sidebar on page 21 for Clyman's firsthand account).

After Clyman finished his needlework on Smith's head, the partisan mounted his horse and rode about a mile to a small stream where the men made camp. Never one to abide sitting around, Smith allowed himself only 10 days to heal before insisting the brigade move lest it be caught by the coming winter. For the remainder of his short life (he was killed by Comanches on the Santa Fe Trail in 1831), Smith wore his hair long to cover his scars.

The Crows welcomed Smith's brigade to their camp, set in a protected valley off Wyoming's Wind River (probably near Dubois). The Indians' hospitality was also shared by another Ashley brigade, which was commanded by John Weber, a former Danish sea captain.

BUILDING THE AMERICAN WEST

July 1, 1825
About 120 fur trappers assemble for the first mountain man rendezvous.

October 26, 1825
The first boats to travel the Erie Canal depart Buffalo, New York, arriving in New York City on November 4.

Summer 1826
William Ashley bows out of the fur trade, selling his interest to Jedediah Smith, David Jackson and Bill Sublette. Their partnership is the forerunner of the Rocky Mountain Fur Company. Thomas Jefferson and John Adams die on July 4.

1827
Astor hires Bernard Pratte & Company, co-owned by Pierre Chouteau, Jr., to manage the American Fur Company's Western Department. The American Fur Company absorbs the Columbia Fur Company into its Western Department as the Upper Missouri Outfit, managed by Kenneth McKenzie.

Charles Bent.

March 26, 1827
German composer Ludwig van Beethoven dies.

May 1827
Colonel Henry Leavenworth establishes Cantonment Leavenworth (eventually renamed Fort Leavenworth) on the Missouri River (today's Eastern Kansas).

1828
Charles Bent forms a trading partnership with his brother, William. Their firm is the forerunner of Bent, St. Vrain & Company.

July 4, 1828
The first U.S. passenger railroad, the Baltimore & Ohio, begins laying track.

Spring 1829
Buffalo robes, dressed by Indian women, sell for $3.00 each in Eastern markets. The American Fur Company ships about 25,000 robes to meet the demand.

Mandan Indians in buffalo robes.

Fall 1829
The American Fur Company begins construction of Fort Union just above the

THE JAWS OF DEATH

JEDEDIAH SMITH MAULED BY A GRIZZLY BEAR.

Jedediah Smith

. . . a large Grssely came down the vally we being in single file men on foot le[a]ding pack horses he struck us about the center then turning ran paralel to our line Capt. [Jedediah] Smith being in the advanc he ran to the open ground and as he immerged from the thicket he and the bear met face to face

Grissly did not hesitate a moment but sprung on the capt taking him by the head first pitc[h]ing sprawling on the earth he gave him a grab by the middle fortunately cat[c]hing by the ball pouch and Butcher K[n]ife which he broke but breaking several of his ribs and cutting his head badly none of us having any surgical Knowledge what was to be done one Said come take hold and he wuld say why not you so it went around I asked Capt what was best he said one or two [go] for water and if you have a needle and thread git it out and sew up my wounds around my head which was bleeding freely I got a pair of scissors and cut off his hair and then began my first Job of d[r]essing wounds upon examination I [found] the bear had taken nearly all his head in his capcious mouth close to his left eye on one side and clos to his right ear on the other and laid the skull bare to near the crown of the head leaving a white streak whare his teeth passed one of his ears was torn from his head out to the outer rim after stitching all the other wounds in the best way I was capabl and according to the captains directions the ear being the last I told him I could do nothing for his Eare O you must try to stich up some way or other said he then I put in my needle stiching it through and through and over and over laying the lacerated parts togather as nice as I could with my hands

–James Clyman, *Journal of a Mountain Man* (Mountain Press Publishing Company).

1821–1840

Missouri River's confluence with the Yellowstone.

1830
While at sea, inventor Samuel Colt comes up with the concept of a revolving firearm.

April 6, 1830
Joseph Smith founds the Mormon Church in Fayette, New York.

1831
Network that frees slaves is dubbed the "Underground Railroad" after steam railroads.

Chief Black Hawk.

1832
The Black Hawk War in Illinois and Wisconsin drives the Sauk and Fox tribes west of the Mississippi River.

March 26, 1832
The American Fur Company's steamboat, Yellow Stone, departs St. Louis for the upper Missouri, eventually reaching Fort Union, just above the mouth of the Yellowstone River. Among her passengers is artist George Catlin.

May 5, 1832
Congress appropriates $12,000 to vaccinate Indians along the Missouri River from smallpox, but bureaucratic indifference and prejudice doom the project to failure.

July 18, 1832
Atsina (a.k.a. Gros Ventre) Indians and members of the Rocky Mountain Fur Company clash in Pierre's Hole (Teton Valley, in Eastern Idaho), following the annual mountain man rendezvous.

November 12–13, 1833
The Leonid meteor shower excites Indians on the Great Plains.

Steamboat Yellow Stone.

June 1834
John Jacob Astor sells his interest in the American Fur Company. On June 1, fur trader William Sublette chooses a site on the Laramie River for his new trading post, Fort William; the post eventually becomes Fort Laramie.

By February 1824, Smith was itching to leave. Outfitted with horses from the Crows, he and his brigade headed west toward the Continental Divide. Heavy snow soon stopped their progress below Union Pass in the Wind River Mountains, forcing a retreat to the Crows' camp. After the trappers returned, the Crows told Smith about another pass a bit south of where he had failed. Although this time Smith's men nearly starved from a lack of game, they succeeded in crossing the Continental Divide on a grade that would eventually prove gentle enough for wagons and play a critical role in America's Westward expansion—South Pass. Others had used South Pass before Smith, but historians credit him for making it known to the public.

Tom Fitzpatrick

West of the Wind River Mountains, in the valley of the Seeds-kee-dee (now known as the Green River), the trappers found a beaver paradise. Smith split his brigade into two groups for trapping, taking command of one and putting the other under Tom Fitzpatrick. The parties agreed to rejoin just east of South Pass on the upper Sweetwater River in mid-June.

Peter Skene Ogden

After harvesting numerous beaver pelts, Fitzpatrick, Clyman and the rest of their company reached the rendezvous site ahead of Smith's. Wanting to send their furs back to St. Louis via boat rather than pack horses, Fitzpatrick and Clyman rode down the Sweetwater about 15 miles to see if the river was navigable. Telling Clyman to scout farther downstream and wait, Fitzpatrick returned to the main camp. By now, Smith's brigade had arrived. Leaving Fitzpatrick in charge of making a bull boat (buffalo hides stretched over a willow frame), Smith rode east to fetch Clyman. Reaching the confluence of the Sweetwater and North Platte Rivers, the partisan found Clyman's camp, but

1849 drawing of Fort Hall.

July 15, 1834
Fur trader Nathaniel Wyeth begins constructing Fort Hall alongside the Snake River in Eastern Idaho.

Autumn 1834
Delmonico's restaurant in New York City offers a three-course meal for 12¢.

November 24, 1835
Texas legislature authorizes the formation of Ranger companies to protect the frontier.

December 29, 1835
The Cherokees are compelled to cede their land in Georgia.

Samuel Colt.

February 25, 1836
Samuel Colt patents a forerunner of his Colt Paterson revolver.

March 2, 1836
Texas declares its independence.

March 6, 1836
Mexican forces commanded by Santa Anna overrun the Alamo after a 13-day siege.

March 19, 1836
Comanches attack Fort Parker, Texas, stealing nine-year-old Cynthia Ann Parker.

April 21, 1836
Texans led by Sam Houston defeat the Mexican Army at San Jacinto.

July 4, 1836
Narcissa Whitman and Eliza Spalding become the first white women to cross the Continental Divide at South Pass.

Santa Anna.

Washington Irving wrote in his classic,* Adventures of Captain Bonneville, *an account of mountain men at a rendezvous: "The three rival companies, which, for a year past had been endeavoring to out-trade, out-trap and out-wit each other, were here encamped in close proximity. . . . The hunting season over, all past tricks and manoeuvres are forgotten, all feuds and bickerings buried in oblivion. . . . This, then, is the trapper's holiday, when he is all for fun and frolic, and ready for a saturnalia among the mountains."

no sign of the trapper, merely fresh tracks from a large Indian war party. Figuring that Clyman's scalp was now decorating some warrior's lodgepole, Smith turned back up the Sweetwater to deliver the bad news.

By now snowmelt in the Wind River Mountains was increasing the Sweetwater's flow.

May 27, 1837
James Butler Hickok is born in Troy Grove, Illinois.

June 19, 1837
The steamboat St. Peter's, infected by smallpox, reaches Fort Clark, launching an epidemic that all but destroys the Mandans.

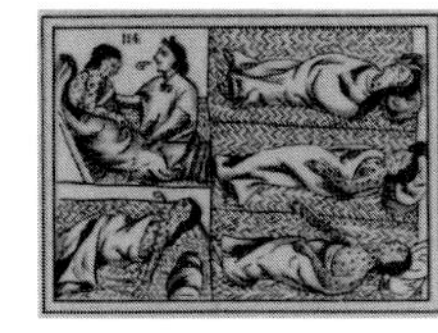

16th-century smallpox illustration.

June 20, 1837
Queen Victoria succeeds to the British throne at age 18.

September 1, 1838
William Clark dies at the age of 68 in St. Louis, Missouri.

October 1838
Upward of 16,000 Cherokees are forcibly removed from their Georgia homes and escorted to the Indian Territory (now Oklahoma) on the Trail of Tears.

Trail of Tears.

1839
Pierre Chouteau, Jr. & Company, a successor firm to the American Fur Company, ships 45,000 buffalo robes to Eastern buyers. The following year, the shipment increases to 67,000. The Republic of Texas begins ordering Colt Paterson revolvers from Samuel Colt.

July 1840
Final rendezvous is held on the Green River (Wyoming), ending the mountain man era.

Pierre Chouteau, Jr.

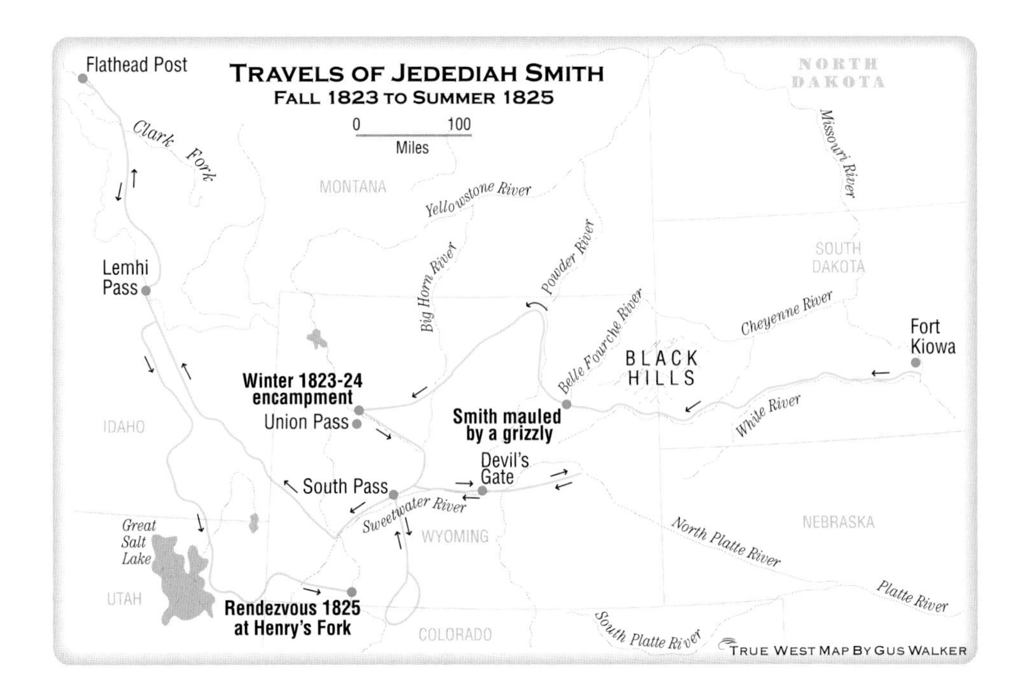

Taking two helpers, Fitzpatrick launched the bull boat and its load of pelts, allowing Smith and the rest of the brigade to continue trapping. Fitzpatrick's instructions were to deliver the furs to William Ashley and then lead him back to the mountains with supplies. The plan called for Ashley's pack train to rendezvous the following summer with the brigades of Smith and John Weber (plus Ashley's other trappers who were operating around the mouth of the Bighorn River in Central Montana) on the Green River or one of its tributaries.

The scheme nearly fell apart when Fitzpatrick's bull boat sank either at a treacherous rapid on the Sweetwater called Devil's Gate or (more likely) in the upper North Platte River. Fitzpatrick and his companions lost two of their rifles and all of their ammunition, but did manage to salvage most of the furs. Unable to kill more buffalo to make another boat, they dug a hole and cached the furs and then started walking toward the Missouri River.

Hungry, but no worse for wear, Fitzpatrick and his two men eventually reached the U.S. Army's Fort Atkinson (north of Omaha, Nebraska). Imagine their shock at seeing Jim Clyman, who had arrived just 10 days earlier.

Clyman had slipped away from the Indian war party that Smith assumed had killed him. Figuring the Indians had wiped out the brigade, Clyman had headed east on foot, following the North Platte toward the Missouri River and safety. He had no way of knowing that Fitzpatrick would soon follow in his footsteps.

Happy to know Clyman was still alive, Fitzpatrick penned a letter with Jedediah Smith's instructions to William Ashley in St. Louis, asking Ashley to meet him at Fort Atkinson with supplies for the brigades that were still in the mountains. Fitzpatrick then borrowed horses and he and the other trappers headed back to retrieve the cached furs.

OREGON TERRITORY

While Fitzpatrick struggled to deliver his cargo of pelts, Jedediah Smith and the remainder of the brigade had recrossed South Pass and renewed their quest for beaver. Keeping together as much as possible for security from Indians, the trappers would separate into two-man teams to work individual streams, then rejoin and move to fresh pickings. Unable to transport all the fur they were harvesting, the mountain men cached their pelts along the way, intending to retrieve them before their rendezvous with Ashley. Game was no problem as long as they had ammunition. Knowing that the Hudson's Bay Company was operating out of Flathead Post on the Clark Fork River (in Western Montana), Smith decided to trap his way north and purchase supplies from the British. For collateral, he would use beaver pelts.

The Oregon Territory, which included the present states of Oregon, Washington, Idaho and parts of Montana and Wyoming, had been jointly administered by Great Britain and the United States since 1818. But in reality, it was a fiefdom of the powerful Hudson's Bay Company. Smith's decision to enter the British realm had a lot of subplots: he needed supplies, yes, but he certainly was eager to get a firsthand look at the British operation that the Americans hated, and he, of course, wanted to make off with as much of their bounty as he could wrangle.

In late summer 1824, the seven-man brigade reached Southeast Idaho (near Blackfoot) where it found signs that other trappers had recently worked the area. Soon the Americans came across a party of Iroquois trappers who were members of a large Hudson's Bay Company trapping brigade headed by Alexander Ross. The Iroquois had separated from Ross' main party to trap the tributaries of the Snake River and had recently had a run-in with the Shoshonis. Wanting protection, the Iroquois paid Smith 105 beaver pelts—all they had—to escort them back to Ross.

When the Americans and Iroquois met up with the Hudson's Bay brigade, Ross wasn't pleased. Not only had Smith garnered furs Ross had hoped to add to his tally, but also the American presence meant the Hudson's Bay Company no longer held a trapping monopoly in the Oregon Territory. Unwilling to murder Smith's party and perhaps rekindle another war between the United States and Great Britain, Ross allowed Smith to accompany him to Flathead Post—six log huts—which they reached on November 26, 1824. The Hudson's Bay factor (trading post commander) was no happier to see the Americans than Ross, but he didn't allow that to stand in the way of business. The factor sold Smith the supplies he needed—paid for in pelts—but at a highly inflated price.

On December 20, less than a month after it had arrived, the Hudson's Bay brigade departed the trading post under its new leader, Peter Skene Ogden. The party included 59 men, 30 Indian women, 35 children, 61 guns, 268 horses and 352 traps. Smith's small brigade followed a couple of days later, loosely attaching itself to the much larger Hudson's Bay outfit for security from Blackfoot war parties, which ranged as far south as the Snake River. Throughout the winter and into spring, the two brigades leapfrogged each other as they strived to clean one stream after another of its beaver.

Sometime that spring, the rival trappers reached Cache Valley (in Northern Utah), where Smith again teamed up with John Weber's brigade, which had wintered there. Upset that the loathed British had invaded what the Americans regarded as their exclusive domain—they were actually below the 42nd parallel, and therefore, on Spanish soil, but no one seemed to notice—a number of Weber's men, led by Johnson Gardner, rode to the Hudson's Bay camp and persuaded many of Ogden's free trappers (men not trapping for wages) to defect, saying Ashley would pay them eight times more for their furs than would the Hudson's Bay Company. Heaping injury on insult, those who defected brought their pelt inventories, robbing Ogden of what he had hoped would be a successful trapping season. Fearing that his entire brigade could desert, Ogden fled north, leaving the field to the Americans. All together, the British lost 23 free trappers (some reports say 29) and 700 furs.

RENDEZVOUS

Meanwhile, William Ashley had acted on Tom Fitzpatrick's letter requesting that he bring supplies to Fort Atkinson so Fitzpatrick could lead him to the summer rendezvous with the trapping brigades. But Ashley's joy over the news of Smith's successful fur harvest was dampened when Andrew Henry unexpectedly quit their partnership. Determined to go it alone, Ashley recruited more trappers, assembled a store of trade goods and horse packers and headed up the Missouri River, reaching the army post on October 21, 1824. Five days later, Fitzpatrick arrived, having retrieved the pelts he had cached following the sinking of his bull boat. By early November, Ashley and his 25-man party with their 50 pack horses were underway. In addition to Tom Fitzpatrick and Jim Clyman, the group included Robert Campbell and James P. Beckwourth, two other individuals destined to leave their mark on the era of the mountain man.

By the end of June 1825, 120 trappers had assembled on Henry's Fork of the Green River (in Southern Wyoming) for the first mountain man rendezvous. In addition to renewing old friendships—imagine Jedediah Smith's reaction to learning that Jim Clyman was alive—the men held shooting and knife-throwing contests, wrestling matches and foot races. The seeds of the future rendezvous celebrations, which have added so much color to the mountain man era, were sown in the first one. But alas, Ashley had failed to bring the one trade item that would have turned the gathering into a bacchanalia—liquor. It was a mistake that would never again be repeated.

On July 1, the trappers swapped their hard-earned beaver pelts for gunpowder, lead, sugar, coffee, tobacco, shaving soap (most Indian women preferred clean-shaven suitors), trade beads, blankets, fishhooks and a host of other truck to see them through the coming year. Having lost Henry as a partner, Ashley needed someone to represent his interests in the field. The choice was easy: Jedediah Smith.

On July 2, Ashley and Smith assembled their entourage of packers and began the long trek to St. Louis. The rendezvous resupply had been a success. It allowed the trappers to remain in the mountains rather than have to sacrifice an entire trapping season by taking their furs to the Eastern markets. The men paid for their trade goods with beaver pelts, valued the first year at $3.00 per pound. Ashley not only earned a profit on the furs that he would sell in St. Louis—that year he returned with nearly 9,000 pounds of pelts worth upwards of $50,000—but also on the trade goods, which he marked up 200, 500, even 1,000 percent above their cost in St. Louis.

During the next 15 years, increasing numbers of trappers would flock to the mountains, lured not only by adventure but also by the promise of wealth. Few would prosper. Some such as Robert Campbell and Bill Sublette would give up the trapper's life and become traders,

FROM MOUNTAIN STREAM TO THE HEAD OF A KING

MAKING BEAVER HATS

After a beaver was trapped and skinned, the trapper, his Indian wife or a trapping brigade camp tender cleaned the flesh off the pelt and stretched it on a willow frame to dry. Dried furs were then compressed in 60- to 90-lb. bales for transport and sale to Eastern or European hat makers.

Beaver pelts contain long guard hairs and soft, barbed underhair. Hatters first removed these guard hairs and then shaved off the underhair. After placing a mound of underhair on a worktable (the amount depending on the hat style and size), the hatter twanged it with a bowstring to spread the hair evenly, which enabled its microscopic barbs to hook onto one another, forming a "batt."

Multiple batts were then layered with wet cloths, from which the batts absorbed moisture. Next, the hatter joined two batts into a "hood" (hat body), and then boiled it for six to eight hours, which made the "hood-felt" tight and compact. After boiling, the hood was placed on a wooden mold and shaped into a hat, be it a Continental tricorn, Navy cocked hat, Wellington, Dorsay or Regent.

If properly cared for, a beaver hat could last a lifetime or longer.

seeing that they could earn a far greater return by brokering beaver and trade goods—including liquor—between the fur brigades and St. Louis. The era of the mountain men lasted but a generation, yet its imprint on the history of the American West exists to this day, helped in large part by the summer revelries that have come to be known as rendezvous.

MOUNTAIN MAN LINGO

TRAPPER TALK

Bourgeois: American trading post commander.

Camp tenders: Fur company employees who cooked and cared for the furs harvested by company trappers.

Clerk: Second in command to a trapping brigade partisan, trading post bourgeois or a factor.

Cordelle: Rope (usually attached to the mast) used to tow keelboats upriver.

Engagé: A fur trapper or trading post laborer who worked for wages.

Factor: A trading post commander working for the North West or Hudson's Bay Companies or the trader at an American Indian factory (government-run trading post).

Foofuraw: Ribbons, beads, bells or other gewgaws that trappers gave as presents to Indian wives or used to purchase sexual favors from Indian women.

Hivernan: Mountain man or trading post employee who had spent at least one winter in the wilds. Hivernans considered themselves superior to mangeurs de lard.

Mangeur de lard: Greenhorn trapping recruits or trading post employees who had never wintered beyond the mouth of the Platte River. The French term means "eater of pork," someone who eats hog instead of buffalo as did a true mountain man.

On the Prairie: Something—usually liquor—given free of charge.

Partisan: Commander of a trapping brigade.

Plew: A beaver pelt.

Trapping brigade: A party of trappers, numbering anywhere from eight to 100 or more, traveling together for security. The men would separate into small trapping teams to work individual streams, then rejoin to move to a different area.

Voyageur: Any man working on a riverboat (other than a steamboat) in the fur trade.

THE ALAMO

WHEN SO MANY GAVE EVERYTHING IN A LOSING CAUSE

IF a single word could define American bravery and grit, could signify the American spirit of defiance, that word would be "Alamo."

IT WAS THE UNLIKELIEST place to carry such weight in American history and to stand so unparalleled in Texan lore: A tiny Spanish mission already over 100 years old in San Antonio that was built for prayer, not battle. An outpost seen as so inconsequential to the emerging Texas—then a state of Mexico but longing to belong to the United States—that two of its heroes were within its walls because they had been sent to blow it up.

But all these years later, what happened at the Alamo over 13 days in the cold February and March of 1836 remains a shining moment in the American character. Historian Lon Tinkle called it *13 Days to Glory* in his compelling book on the siege of the Alamo.

This conflict, of course, had been years in the making as Texas found itself in dispute with the governments to both its south and its north: The United States wouldn't take it and the Mexicans wouldn't let it go.

Many Americans thought Texas had been included in the 1803 Louisiana Purchase, but that was a fluke, since Spain, not France, controlled Texas. Then in 1819, the United States signed a treaty with Spain, taking Florida in exchange for giving up any claim to Texas.

You can imagine the howls over that decision. Come 1822, Mexico finally gained its independence from Spain, but Mexico had no interest in giving up Texas and twice rebuffed American offers to buy it. But Mexico made a concession that would be its undoing—it welcomed American settlers who would live under Mexico's laws. Stephen F. Austin led settlers to the new country and in just 15 years, they did remarkable things: blunted the Native Americans who had long vexed the Spanish and Mexicans, attracted 30,000 Anglo-Americans and made the land produce like never before.

Alamo defenders entered the mission with hope. They were heroes to fight for Texas independence, but none truly thought reinforcements would fail to save the day.

Mexico quickly saw the threat of land-hungry Americans, which one Mexican newspaper called a parasite that "devours Mexican entrails," while another decried the "fanatical intolerance" of Americans for non-whites. In 1830, amidst these public concerns, Mexico prohibited further immigration. By then, it was too late. There were too many settlers; they were too successful; they held title to too much land. When the government in Mexico City imposed taxes on Texas produce, but didn't even dignify Texans with their own state (making them share statehood with Coahuila), the Texans viewed it very much as the early colonists had viewed the tea tax that led to the Boston Tea Party.

And then Santa Anna became President of Mexico and turned into a despot, dissolving the legislatures, abandoning the 1824 constitution and making it clear

Sent by Sam Houston, James Bowie (right) and William Barret Travis (above) were to "destroy the fortifications of the city" and decided against it. In their eyes, the Alamo was the "key to Texas."

he'd never let Texas go. (When Stephen Austin went to Mexico City to appeal for statehood, he was not only rebuffed, but thrown in a Mexican prison for 18 months. He was released just six months before the Alamo siege. Santa Anna believed Austin would be so intimidated by his imprisonment, he would advise submission to Mexico, which shows the general was a lousy judge of character.)

It was obvious what had to be done, and when the Texans started fighting back, they showed themselves to be one helluva ragtag army. They took the Alamo in December 1835 by defeating Santa Anna's brother-in-law, General Cos. In losing it three months later, they would usher in Texas independence.

From Washington-on-the-Brazos, as Texans optimistically called their capital, two men were sent to the Alamo with the express purpose of blowing it up. One was Jim Bowie, commanding a group of volunteers. The other was Lt. Colonel William Barret Travis, of the Texas Army. The two men would agree on almost nothing over the next couple of months, but they did agree not to destroy the crumbling mission that they saw as the "key to Texas."

The twenty-seven-year-old Travis was a young buck eager to make his mark. He was a lawyer who had abandoned his wife and children in Alabama but now was newly engaged and had custody of his young son. He saw himself as the true commander at the fort, being its only real officer. But he didn't command the loyalty of the volunteers, who voted to put Bowie in charge, and so the uncomfortable—and mostly unworkable—compromise was that they would equally hold command.

Travis saw Bowie as a naive drunk. Travis refused to believe Santa Anna would advance on the Alamo in the middle of winter. He was under the mistaken impression that the dried grasses would never feed Santa Anna's horses. When Bowie explained that horses preferred the dried winter grass, Travis looked at him as if he were an idiot. Nor did Travis respect that Bowie had an intimate knowledge of Mexican culture and life, seeing him suspiciously as a "Mexican lover."

The forty-year-old Bowie was a widower by then, having lost his small children and loving wife to the plague. She had been such a beautiful woman, this "Castilian lady" from one of Mexico's fine old families. He was still heartsick and still looking for a grounding. He stayed "roaring drunk" most of the time, either by choice or grief. He was also sick, perhaps with tuberculosis, although he'd never admit it, but the racking cough gave him away. Bowie was best known for wielding his knife, but his personal claim to fame was that he held title to a million acres of Texas land. He had come to the Alamo to protect his empire. He resented the young, wet-behind-the-ears Travis trying to tell him what to do and ignoring his sage advice.

These two men would become legends because of the Alamo. Some historians argue that they might not have been remembered for much without it.

The third legendary figure from this saga would have been famous even if he hadn't died at the Alamo. He was perhaps the best of the 182 men who would fall at the hands of an enormous army commanded by a vain man who considered himself the Napoleon of the West.

Davy Crockett was already a national legend when he arrived with his glib tongue, coonskin cap and "Old Betsy" rifle. By then, he'd already served in the Tennessee Legislature and the United States Congress and was a darling of the media that hung on his homespun stories. He took to calling the advancing general "Santy Anny," and vowed his men would hold whatever position he was given.

Whether Davy Crockett died fighting, or was captured and executed by Santa Anna's men, is still hotly debated.

The Mexican Army showed up the morning of February 23, 1836. It was a balmy 60-degree day. Bowie wasn't too surprised to see them. Travis was stunned. For hours that morning, there had been a strange sound in the Plaza of the surrounding town. "A low rumble at first, hardly more than a whisper, it had grown in intensity to a roar, until it rattled in the ears and jolted the dreams of all who heard," Tinkle writes. It was the sound of the Mexican families leaving town, the same families that had danced and drunk and eaten the last few nights with the soldiers and volunteers in one fandango after another. There'd been George Washington's birthday to celebrate and when another excuse didn't manifest itself, life to celebrate. But now, through the hangovers, came the sound of all those creaking wheels and cries of oxen as the Mexicans left, wondering why in the world the Texans were staying.

As the civilians left, Santa Anna camped nearby with an army of 1,500 (including hundreds of pack mules, 300 two-wheel carts and a crate of prized fighting cocks.

Travis immediately sent a messenger to get reinforcements. There were other armies nearby—Col. James Fannin had more than 400 men not far away in Goliad. Surely, help was on its way, as nearby a sea of red and blue Mexican uniforms practiced maneuvers.

But there never would be reinforcements. Fannin would decide the Alamo was doomed, so there wasn't anything to do. Texans gathered at the makeshift capital were declaring independence and celebrating Sam Houston's birthday, which was no accident. Other Texans wanted to rush to the aid of the Alamo, but Houston convinced them not to go and instead stay to create the framework of government. He would later say it was the hardest decision he ever made, but history isn't sure he was sincere. Tinkle seems to think the man was so self-centered, the birthday celebrations were more important than the men fighting against impossible odds at the Alamo.

For 12 days, Santa Anna's men shot their cannons at the old fort, sniped at the men inside and for 12 days not a single casualty was suffered inside the Alamo.

Among the legends from those days is the one that says Travis took his sword and drew a line in the dirt. "I now want every man who is determined to stay here and die with me to cross the line." It's said that every man but one crossed that line; that Bowie was carried over the mark on his sickbed cot. But while it's a great story—and there's evidence Travis did give his men a pep talk—the source of the line-in-the-sand story eventually admitted he had made it up.

"Travis had watched helplessly the ebb of spirits in his men as the Mexican night sorties and cannonade had wrecked their nerves and sleep for almost two weeks," Tinkle writes about the 13th day. "Morale was not low, but sheer fatigue had left the men hollow-eyed and testy. On the first few nights, the exhilaration of danger and the hope of early relief had cancelled out weariness. The 182 men guarding an expanse that required a thousand for properly rotated watches all felt they could get what rest they needed and restore their stamina once General Fannin and his four hundred men got there. It was only as hope dimmed that the nights began to seem endless. Willpower alone kept eyes open, senses alert. They had no coffee in the Alamo; whatever other stimulants they might have salvaged had long since been consumed."

Santa Anna, having himself a honeymoon with a town beauty, was well aware of the conditions inside the Alamo. That's why he stopped shelling the afternoon of the 12th day—giving the "lawless foreigners," as he saw them, a time to sleep. He knew that before they awoke, he would have his men on the move. He gave the order for his troops to be ready to attack at 4 A.M.

"Three startling and separate sounds roused the Texans into wakefulness," Tinkle recounts. "They occurred almost simultaneously. A blast from a bugle lifted the Mexican infantry to its feet from the cold ground. At once there began from each of the four columns on the four sides of the fortress a wild rush of humanity. The piercing bugle blast was as nothing compared to the second sound—the drumming of thousands of feet on the hard ground. Beside Santa Anna there now poured forth into the frozen air the third sound, most fearful of all. Santa Anna's regimental band burst forth with the notes of an ancient Moorish battle march, the famed *deguello* signal that no quarter would be given. It was the musical equivalent of the red flag of no mercy."

The battle song that became Santa Anna's personal battle signature, meant "to slit the throat."

On the first wave of assault, the Texans felled so many Mexican soldiers, that some ran

One of the most mythologized images of the Alamo. We now know this never happened—not only because Zuber, the original tale teller, admitted his story was false. Logically, it made no sense. Why would Travis draw the line and drain his men of hope?

away, screaming "Diablos! Diablos!" But the attacks kept coming, even as the Texans inflicted staggering losses.

The Mexicans finally breached the Alamo walls, pouring into the courtyard where many would die in hand-to-hand combat.

The sounds of the battle had to be astonishing, Tinkle writes. "The crashing noise of shattering walls, the human cries, the roar of guns were thunderous in the small area. If the bells of San Fernando church had rung at six o'clock that morning, they could not have been heard."

Travis was perhaps among the first killed inside the fort, shot in the head. Bowie was killed in the baptistry, where his cot had been put. His Mexican sister-in-law, among the civilians who survived that day, would tell of seeing his body pitched on bayonets, but there were no eyewitnesses to his death.

The story of how Davy Crockett died has changed dramatically over the last century and a half. For most of that time, we visualized his final moments as depicted in the 1903 painting by Robert Jenkins Onderdonk: in his fringed buckskins and coonskin cap, he wields his flintlock rifle over his head like a club as the Mexicans advance. Some, including Tinkle, have written about the fury of his death—taking out many before he himself fell, lying amidst a pile of Mexican dead.

But that image changed dramatically in the mid-1950s with the publication of a "diary" allegedly written in 1836 by a man who said he had witnessed Davy's execution after the battle. José Enrique de la Peña, an aide to one of Santa Anna's colonels, said after the fighting stopped, seven prisoners were brought before the general, who showed no mercy. Among them was "naturalist David Crockett, well known in North America for his unusual adventures." Most historians now believe this is how Davy died, including *True West* magazine's contributing editor and Alamo expert Paul Hutton.

Even after all the men at the Alamo were dead—some men "cut loose" and were killed outside the walls—the shooting continued and then the mutilation of the bodies began. Santa Anna directed that the Texans be burned, denying them a Christian burial. He had his surviving soldiers separate the Mexican dead for a decent burial. His dead and wounded numbered about 600.

But the Mexican victory would be short-lived. All of Texas was shaken by the news of the slaughter at the Alamo. It was repeated just a week later when Santa Anna trapped Gen. Fannin's troops at Goliad, held them for a week and then massacred them all. "What he did finally was to galvanize Texas into a mighty resistance," Tinkle writes.

On April 21, Santa Anna stupidly wandered into a trap at San Jacinto, near Galveston, that had been set by Sam Houston. In just 20 minutes, with the cries of "Remember the Alamo" and "Remember Goliad" filling the air, the Mexican president was captured and Texan independence was assured.

As Tinkle puts it, "The Alamo that began in defeat ended in resurrection."

THE SADDEST, MOST COURAGEOUS LETTER THAT WAS NEVER ANSWERED

TO THE PEOPLE OF TEXAS AND ALL AMERICANS IN THE WORLD—Fellow citizens—& compatriots—I am besieged by a thousand or more of the Mexicans under Santa Anna.—I have sustained a continual bombardment and connonade for 24 hours & have not lost a man—the enemy has demanded a surrender at discretion, otherwise the garrison are to be put to the sword if the fort is taken—I have answered the demand with a cannon shot, and our flag still waves proudly from the walls—I shall never surrender or retreat. Then, I call on you in the name of Liberty, of patriotism & everything dear to the American character, to come to our aid with all dispatch—The enemy is receiving reinforcement daily & will no doubt increase to three or four thousand in four or five days. If this call is neglected, I am determined to sustain myself as long as possible & die like a soldier who never forgets what is due to his own honor & that of his country—VICTORY OR DEATH.

P.S. The Lord is on our side—when the enemy appeared in sight we had not three bushels of corn—We have since found in deserted houses 80 or 90 bushels & got into the walls 20 or 30 head of beeves.

—Written by Lt. Colonel William Travis on February 24, 1836.

HOW DID DAVY REALLY DIE?

DID DAVY CROCKETT GO DOWN SWINGING OR SURRENDERING?

JUST *after midnight, on March 6, 1836, Gen. Santa Anna orders his 2,064 troops to move toward their assault positions. Select* soldados *(soldiers) stealthily sneak up on the Tejano sentries, who lie in dugouts positioned away from the Alamo, and slit the guards' throats.*

JUST BEFORE SUNRISE (around 5 A.M.) a *soldado* from the second column yells out "Viva Santa Anna!" His comrades echo the cry. Furious that he has lost the element of surprise, Santa Anna orders his musicians to sound the attack. A rocket battery fires the signal to start the assault.

Four separate Mexican columns surge out of the darkness toward the shadowed walls of the Alamo. Awakened by the shouts, the Texans quickly man their cannons and commence a furious enfilade fire from the church and corral batteries, forcing the attackers coming in from the east to move north.

Musket and cannon fire pour from the walls of the Alamo, and three attacking columns stall at the north wall. The Texans are holding their own and laying down a deadly fire.

Momentum lost, Santa Anna commits his reserves. *Grenidiers* (grenadiers) and *zapadores* (sappers) charge into the fight and finally succeed in breaching the Texan defense. At the same time, the *cazzadores* (light infantrymen) breach the Alamo's southwest corner from the west side. The Texans fighting there are quickly overwhelmed and fall back, taking refuge in the adobe apartments, convent and church. Mexican troops pour into the compound unchecked, while others seize the abandoned batteries, turn them around and fire at the retreating Texans with their own cannons.

Hand-to-hand combat is fierce, and the fighting turns especially bloody as the Mexican troops go room to room, overwhelming each pocket of resistance and shooting and bayoneting everything that moves.

Some 60 defenders break out of the Alamo, heading east on Gonzales Road, but Santa Anna's cavalry is waiting and cuts them down.

An hour after the initial attack, Davy Crockett stands alone, still proudly and tenaciously defending his diminished position. A frightful gash angles across his forehead. Holding the barrel of his shattered rifle in his right hand and a Bowie knife dripping with blood in his left, Crockett faces his attackers with the courage of a lion. Twenty dead or dying Mexicans lay beneath his buckskin-clad feet.

The man from Tennessee crouches, daring his attackers to take him. As they move in for the kill, Davy swings wildly with everything he has, until he finally falls, fighting with savage ferocity to his last dying breath. The fight is over.

This 1834 print of David Crockett is based on a lost oil painting by Samuel Osgood.

WELL, NOT EXACTLY

That's how we in the United States celebrated the death of "The King of the Wild Frontier" for a good part of the twentieth century. Exemplifying the Texas creed that you have no business telling a story unless you can improve it, David's death scenario just kept growing each time the story was retold. (He referred to himself as David, says Alamo historian Alan C. Huffines, who was also a military advisor for Touchstone Pictures' 2004 *The Alamo*.)

Then, in 1955, at the height of the Disney Davy's fame, a purported memoir from Mexico surfaced that had the audacity to claim Crockett had surrendered. It wasn't until an

English translation was released in 1975 that the José Enrique de la Peña memoir was belittled and rebuked. But as historians took a closer look at corroborating evidence, Crockett's dramatic finale began to change.

Let's take a look at the historical record:

David Crockett fights to the end in this old print, while to his left, James Bowie lies on a pallet.

ANGLO ACCOUNTS

One of the first official reports of the Alamo fight comes from Gen. Sam Houston, writing to the commander at Goliad, March 11, 1836: "After the fort was carried, seven men surrendered and called for Santa Anna and quarter. They were murdered by his order."

Although Houston doesn't name Crockett, contemporary newspapers report from the beginning that a group of Alamo defenders had surrendered.

Here's a condensed version of one of the first news reports that appeared in the *Morning Courier & New-York Enquirer*, July 9, 1836:

"Six Americans were discovered near the wall yet unconquered. They were surrounded and ordered by General Castrillón to surrender, which they did under a promise of protection."

One of the six steps forward with "a bold demeanor." The troops notice his "firmness and his noble bearing." Undaunted, "David Crockett" steps forward boldly to face Gen. Santa Anna and looks him "steadfastly in the face."

"His Excellency," Manuel Fernandez Castrillón says to his commander. "Sir, here are six prisoners I have taken alive; how shall I dispose of them?"

Santa Anna looks at Castrillón fiercely and replies, "Have I not told you before how to dispose of them? Why do you bring them to me?"

Several junior officers pull their swords and lunge at Crockett and the others, the Mexicans plunging their swords into "the bosoms of their defenseless prisoners."

MEXICAN ACCOUNTS

Ramón Martínez Caro, Santa Anna's personal secretary, reports in an 1837 pamphlet published in Mexico that "there were five who were discovered by General Castrillón while the soldiers stepped out of their ranks and set upon the prisoners until they were all killed."

José Enrique de la Peña's memoir offers a somewhat different version: "some seven men had survived the general carnage and, under the protection of General Castrillón, they were brought before Santa Anna. Among them . . . was the naturalist David Crockett, well known in North America for his unusual adventures . . . Santa Anna answered Castrillón's intervention in Crockett's behalf with a gesture of indignation and, addressing himself to . . . the troops closest to him, ordered his execution. The commanders and officers were outraged at this action and did not support the order . . . but several officers who were around the president and who, perhaps, had not been present during the moment of danger . . . thrust themselves forward . . . and with swords in hand, fell upon these unfortunate, defenseless men just as a tiger leaps upon his prey. Though tortured before they were killed, these unfortunates, died without complaining and without humiliating themselves before their torturers."

AFTERMATH: ODDS & ENDS

Although the David Crockett surrender scenario is still contentious, especially in Texas, Dan Kilgore (author of *How Did Davy Die?*) concludes, "Four officers and a sergeant—all of whom participated in the assault and observed the final tragedy—specifically identified Crockett as one of the captives." Kilgore adds, "Their accounts have come to light over a long period of time, several having surfaced only recently. Any one of them, standing alone, could be subject to question, but considered as a whole, the statements provide stronger documentation than can be claimed for any other incident during the battle."

Others believe Crockett didn't even die at the Alamo. In 1840, William White wrote a letter printed in the *Austin City Gazette* that reported a visit to Guadalajara, Mexico, where a native stated a Texas prisoner had been forced to work in a mine. The enslaved miner was, of course, Crockett. White claimed that Crockett had written a letter to his family in Tennessee and asked White to mail it for him. Even though the letter never arrived, David's son, John Crockett (a congressman from Tennessee), allegedly started for Mexico to search for his father.

"Too much has been made over the details of how David died at the Alamo. Such details are not important. What is important is that he died as he had lived. His life was one of indomitable bravery; his death was a death of intrepid courage. His life was one of wholehearted dedication to his concepts of liberty. He died staking his life against what he regarded as intolerable tyranny," wrote James A. Shackford in his 1955 book, *David Crockett.*

The earliest known photograph of the Alamo is this daguerreotype, which was taken prior to 1850.

LUCK OF THE DRAW

PRISONERS' FATE DETERMINED BY BLACK BEAN LOTTERY

GENERAL *Santa Anna ordered every single Texan prisoner executed—men, fighting for the Republic of Texas.*

A TOTAL OF 214 OF THEM had been captured in December 1842 on the south bank of the Rio Grande in Mier, Tamaulipas, Mexico. The Mexican Army then marched them south to Salado, where the Texans decided they had gone "far enough if not too far into the country."

The Texans had been retaliating for Mexican attacks around San Antonio, known then as West Texas, and the capture of their fellow Texans by Mexican Gen. Adrian Woll's 1,400-man army, which seized the city on September 11, 1842. Alarmed by the invasion, Texans rushed to form volunteer militias. Texans under Gen. Alexander Somervell soon marched south, capturing Laredo and Guerrero, but abandoned their mission on December 19, 1842, when the general decided it was too late to catch Woll. About 300 men refused to retreat and instead crossed the Rio Grande on Christmas Day and attacked the Mexican border town of Mier. Even though they had lost only 30 men to the Mexican's 600, the Texans surrendered because they were low on ammunition.

After spending almost two months in prison, the Texans escaped on February 11, 1843. The escapees disarmed 150 Mexican infantrymen, killed a number of guards, stole horses and put the Mexican cavalry to flight.

Unfortunately, most of the Texans then got lost. Bigfoot Wallace described their plight under the scorching sun: "the suffering of men became so intolerable that many of them, to relieve themselves of all superfluous weight, threw away their guns and equipment. . . . Many of the men gave out entirely, and laid down by the wayside to die. . . . Still the rest of us struggled on, hoping that our strength might hold out until we came to water."

They finally got their drink of water, but it was after accidentally wandering into a camp of Mexican soldiers. Within days of their escape, 176 Texans were recaptured and sent back to prison, where they learned of Mexico President Santa Anna's wrath.

THE BRUCE OF THE WEST

Luckily for some, Coahuila Gov. Francisco Mexia refused to carry out Santa Anna's ordered execution, and several foreign ministers to Mexico got the decree modified to more humane terms: that only one man in 10 be executed. In an earthen pot were placed 159 white beans and 17 black. Prison commander Col. Dominic Huerta had the Texans chained in pairs and blindfolded. They were marched out as an officer approached with the *olla* containing the beans. For a few moments, the Texans stood silent, and then the drawing began.

The jar was held up, so no one could see inside. The officers drew first. Eager to kill Capt. Ewen Cameron, once hailed as the Bruce of the West, the Mexicans had put all the black beans on the top, and made Cameron lead off. They had a reason to want the Scottish-born Cameron dead: he was the kind to persevere.

During the battle at Mier, when the Mexican soldiers had charged at Cameron, he emptied his rifles into them and then threw rocks, forcing the *soldados* to take cover until he could reload.

"Boys, it is no use for us to continue the fight."

During the second day of fighting, a majority of the Texans voted to surrender and laid their guns in the

This illustration, "Shooting the Decimated Texans," appeared in the 1845* Journal of the Texian Expedition Against Mier, *written by Gen. Thomas J. Green. As punishment for the Texans' escape from the Hacienda del Salado, 17 prisoners were executed.

street. Cameron, however, rushed back to his position and urged his men to keep fighting. Some 50 of them stood their ground. Cameron's unit held its position until Cameron saw that all hope was gone. He looked around at his men and said, "Boys, it is no use for us to continue the fight; they are all gone but us." Only then did he break his sword and surrender.

So the Mexicans knew Cameron was tough.

BUILDING THE AMERICAN WEST

1843
Fur trader Joseph Robidoux III plats a town around his Blacksnake Hills trading post, giving rise to St. Joseph, Missouri. Mountain men Jim Bridger and Louis Vasquez open Fort Bridger (Southwestern Wyoming), the first trading post built specifically to supply emigrants on the Oregon Trail. The Hudson's Bay Company establishes Fort Victoria on Vancouver Island. William H. Prescott's three-volume *History of the Conquest of Mexico* is published.

Frank James is born.

January 10
Outlaw Frank James is born.

January 11
Francis Scott Key, author of "The Star-Spangled Banner," dies in Baltimore, Maryland.

May 4
Secretary of State Daniel Webster resigns over the annexation of the Republic of Texas.

May 22
The first major emigrant wagon train leaves Independence, Missouri, bound for Oregon.

May 29
Explorer John C. Fremont and his guide Kit Carson embark on their 14-month journey through the Snake and Columbia River Valleys, and California's San Joaquin Valley.

Secretary of State Daniel Webster resigns.

June 15
The Republic of Texas and Mexico declare a truce.

July 5
Settlers in Champoeg, Oregon, adopt the Organic Law—based on the laws of Iowa—until the United States establishes the Oregon Territory.

"BETTER LUCK NEXT TIME"

"I do not wish to starve and be shot too."

But now one of Cameron's men suspected the Mexicans had rigged the beans against their commander. So, when Cameron approached the jug, he was warned, "Dip deep, Captain." Cameron plunged his hand to the bottom and pulled out a white bean. The Mexicans were disappointed.

The rest of the drawing was done in alphabetical order and went rapidly. Although the men knew that 17 of them would die, they could not help showing their joy as friend after friend drew a life-saving white bean.

And they showed their sorrow, too, as someone who had fought beside them drew a black bean. To these unfortunates, the Mexicans sarcastically wished them "Better luck next time."

As the list dwindled down to the W's, there were two black beans and four white beans left.

Bigfoot Wallace, who'd rushed to Texas after losing a brother and cousin in the Goliad Massacre, had been watching as the beans were drawn, and he thought that the black beans were a little larger than the white ones. When his turn came, he scooped up two beans and felt them between his fingers while a Mexican officer told him to hurry up. Wallace finally dropped one bean and pulled out the other. It was white.

The next two men to draw, Martin Wing and Henry Whalen, both drew black beans. Those were the last of the black beans, and the final three men on the list did not draw. The condemned men were immediately separated from the others and given a chance to write home.

THE SURPRISE "DEATHS"

After drawing a fatal bean, Whalen reportedly said, "Well, they don't make much off me, anyhow, for I know I have killed twenty-five of the yellow-bellies." Whalen then asked the Mexicans for a good last meal, saying, "I do not wish to starve and be shot too." Surprisingly, the Mexicans gave him a double ration, which he ate with great enjoyment and then declared himself ready to die.

1843

July 24
Abel Upshur is appointed Secretary of State, and unlike Daniel Webster, he favors the annexation of Texas.

August 23
Mexican Gen. Santa Anna warns the United States that the annexation of Texas would be a declaration of war against Mexico.

First emigrant train leaves Missouri.

November 28
Hawaii's independence is officially recognized by the British and French Governments.

September
London's weekly magazine, *The Economist*, is launched.

October
Most of the pioneers who departed Missouri in the spring arrive in Oregon.

Charles Dickens'* A Christmas Carol *was so popular that it was often performed as a play.

October 13
Jewish service organization B'nai B'rith is founded in New York City.

December 9
Illustrator John Horsley creates the first Christmas card, which reads: "A Merry Christmas and a Happy New Year to you."

December 17
Charles Dickens' *A Christmas Carol* is published.

"Tell my mother not to grieve for me . . ."

At about 6:30 P.M. on March 25, 1843, nine of the condemned were chained together and shot. The remaining eight were then executed in the same manner. In all, the killing took roughly 11 minutes.

Henry Whalen "received fifteen shots before life was extinct" and continued cursing the Mexicans until someone blew out his brains with a pistol.

The following morning, as the Mexicans prepared to bury the bodies in a mass grave, one corpse was discovered missing. Seventeen-year-old James L. Shepherd had been only wounded, and under cover of darkness, he escaped. Three days later, he was captured in Saltillo and fatally shot.

CHAINED TO FATE

The remaining Texans left Salado on March 26, first marching to San Luis Potosi and then toward Mexico City.

On April 24, the prisoners arrived at Huehuetoca. On Santa Anna's orders, Cameron was taken from his companions at midnight and shot the next morning.

When the prisoners arrived in Mexico City, they were compelled to build a four-mile road to Santa Anna's palace at Tacubaya. They spent six months completing the road, before being moved to Santiago Prison and then back to Perote Prison.

For 18 months, Santa Anna teased Texas President Sam Houston with the prisoners, first offering to free them, and then finding some new reason to keep them in chains. On September 12, 1844, Santa Anna finally issued an order for their release. Of the 261 men who had fought in Mier, 84 died, 35 escaped and 142 were eventually set free.

Former prisoner Thomas Jefferson Green moved to California in 1849 and served in California's first Senate, sponsoring the bill that created the University of California. He later became major general in the California militia.

Bigfoot Wallace had a long, distinguished career as a scout and Texas Ranger.

Samuel Walker joined Jack Hays' company of Rangers in 1844. During one fight, Walker and 14 other Rangers used the new Colt Paterson revolvers to successfully defeat 80 Comanches. Walker then joined Gen. Zachary Taylor's army as a scout, fighting in the battle of Monterrey in September 1846. In October, he visited Samuel Colt, proposing improvements, including a fixed trigger and guard, to Colt's Paterson revolver. The new six-shooter was aptly named the Walker Colt.

As for the condemned men, one of them, James Masterson Ogden, left behind a farewell letter that speaks to the courage of the Texas soldiers.

"Tell my mother not to grieve for me," he wrote, "for the friend that I love is with me and my God will not forsake me.

"Give my love to all . . . and tell them to meet me in heaven.

"I am indebted for the favor of dying with my hands untied. Farewell, all farewell."

DEAD IN THE WATER

OR SO THEY THOUGHT

LATE in the afternoon of May 1, 1846, a band of heavily armed Mexican bandits herded 22 American men, women and children to the edge of a steep bank overlooking the Arroyo Colorado River in South Texas. The Americans were curtly ordered to strip.

TWO LEADERS OF THE AMERICAN PARTY, brothers Anderson and William Rogers, knew what the order meant: the Mexicans intended to kill them and did not want their valuable clothing stained with blood.

The brothers pleaded with the bandit chief, Juan Antonio Baillie, to spare the women and children, but he ignored them and repeated his order, then had his men bind the hands of his naked captives.

Abruptly, Baillie knocked Anderson Rogers to his knees. Drawing a knife, the bandit seized the man by his hair and slit his throat from ear to ear. Baillie methodically moved to the next man as other Mexicans cut the throats of the women and children.

A stunned William Rogers saw his executioner approach, felt fingers grab his hair and wrench back his head. William felt searing pain as the knife ripped his throat before he fell forward and lost consciousness.

General Zachary Taylor and the American "Army of Anticipation" waited at Fort Brown, Texas, for the Mexican War to begin, unaware that Mexican bandits were murdering Americans.

Baillie ordered the 22 bodies untied and thrown in the river. But not all the Americans were dead. When William hit the cold water, the shock revived him. Unbelievably, he still lived. The blade had sliced through his windpipe but had not severed the vital carotid artery or jugular vein.

Directly above him, Mexicans were throwing more bodies over the steep bank. William looked for a place to hide. He found a hole in the side of the clay bank—a washout scoured by tidal currents—and clung there, trembling, as his dead companions dropped into the water beside him and floated downstream.

He was the only survivor. And his party had been such easy pickings.

The Americans had left Corpus Christi five days earlier, on April 25. Twenty-five-year-old William and his brother were sutlers who supplied necessities to army troops. Their wagon train was loaded with food, clothing and utensils that were eagerly awaited by the soldiers. The group had expected no trouble on its trail through the South Texas wilderness and so was poorly armed. On May 1, they had reached the Arroyo Colorado River and forded it at a spot near present-day Harlingen. Forty miles south lay the safety of Fort Brown, where Brownsville is now situated. They walked only four more miles before Baillie and his bandits ambushed them.

Outmanned, outgunned and encumbered with noncombatants (including three women and four children), the men knew their situation was hopeless. When Baillie promised decent treatment in return for their surrender, they accepted. Baillie turned the wagons back to the river, explaining he wanted to camp there for the night. Instead, that is where he stripped and murdered his victims.

All but one.

William cowered along the riverbank, clutching the gaping gash in his throat and trembling from shock and loss of blood. Above him, the killers noisily loaded the wagons and left shortly after dark, going south toward the Rio Grande.

When he was sure they were gone, William crawled up the riverbank and searched for clothing, food or something he could fashion as a weapon. But the bandits had been thorough. They had left nothing.

William considered his choices, and none looked good.

He couldn't go back to Corpus Christi, because it was 200 miles to the northeast. He couldn't go south because that's where the bandits had gone. If they caught him again, they wouldn't fail a second time in killing him. The closest American settlement was Fort Brown, where Gen. Zachary Taylor's "Army of Anticipation" was waiting. But William feared risking capture on the main road, so he struck out across the trackless brush country.

The brush country was a tangle of head-high prickly pear cactus, thorny mesquite, saw grass and greasewood—a haven for rattlesnakes, a hunting ground for cougars and wolves and a barrier to travelers for centuries. William now plunged into it, protected by nothing but his fierce will to live.

Walking slowly in the darkness, he used a mesquite branch as a staff. He pushed it in front of him to part the skin-shredding greasewood and to hold aside the waving fronds of cat-clawed ocotillo. But despite his care, his feet and legs were soon stabbed raw.

As a further torment, clouds of mosquitoes swarmed on his unprotected hide. He beat at them until he was exhausted and his skin was on fire.

Near midnight, he stumbled upon a pond filled by spring rains. To escape the mosquitoes, he threw himself into the water and lay submerged, except for his gashed windpipe. Night travel, he decided, was too difficult. He stayed in the pond until dawn, when the mosquitoes disappeared.

At the break of day, William crawled out and found a mudhole. He wallowed in it, plastering himself with mud. He also piled mud on top of his head to serve as a hat. It worked until the mud dried and flaked away. Soon, William's fair skin reddened. His back and neck burned first, then the rest of his body. His skin blackened, cracked, oozed and burned again.

Blowflies, attracted by the blood oozing from his cut throat, buzzed about his head. Unable to beat them off, he took clay from a creek bank and packed it into the wound. This kept out most of the flies, but some managed to lay their eggs in his flesh. Soon maggots were squirming in the wound, eating the decaying flesh at its raw edges.

On the morning of the second day, May 3, William found himself staggering across a featureless plain of knee-high grass. The absence of landmarks worried him, but then he heard a distant rumbling. He recognized the sound as cannon fire from Fort Brown. One of the earliest battles of the Mexican War had begun.

Guided by the gunfire, William pushed on, struggling through hostile terrain. Hunger plagued him, but he found blackberries abundantly growing in the damp soil beside creek banks. When he tried to eat them, the juice and chewed berries dribbled from the hole in his throat. He solved his problem by lying on his back so the food passed down the back of his throat and entered his stomach. The same technique worked for swallowing water.

Corpus Christi, Texas, where William Rogers lived out his life after being freed from the Mexicans.

All day May 4, William plodded doggedly south on torn, bleeding feet. The gunfire from Fort Brown grew steadily louder. By the end of the day, he had drawn close enough to distinguish the individual reports of the guns.

The next morning, he barely got to his feet. Still he drove himself forward. By noon, he was crawling on his hands and knees.

Less than a mile from Fort Brown, William crept into a Mexican peasant's brush hut and collapsed. For a week, the paisano cleaned William's wounds, bandaged his throat, nursed him and then turned him over to the Mexican authorities in Matamoros, across the river. William was clapped into jail but was later released in a prisoner exchange with the U.S. Army at Fort Brown.

When William was well enough to travel, the army sent a boat to Port Isabel to fetch him back to Corpus Christi. He settled there, married a young widow and fathered eight children. Many of his grandchildren and great-grandchildren still live in South Texas. William devoted his life to ranching, real estate and merchandising. He became a member of the Texas Legislature, vice president of the Corpus Christi, San Diego and Rio Grande Railroad and a member of Pioneer Fire Company Number 1. And he always wore a goatee to hide the terrible scar on his throat.

William never forgot nor forgave the bandits who had injured him so cruelly. He made inquiries and learned the name of the bandit leader. He habitually rode the ferry across the Rio Grande between Brownsville and the Mexican town of Matamoros in order to look among the passengers for Baillie. The story goes that William spotted Baillie one night and lured him to the stern of the ferry, before cutting Baillie's throat and pushing his body overboard. William neither confirmed nor denied it.

In 1877, lung and throat complications arising from his wound led to William's death. He is buried in Corpus Christi.

THE REAL WILD BILL

PRINCE OF THE PISTOLEERS

"WILD BILL," *declared Gen. George Armstrong Custer in 1872, "was a Plainsman in every sense of the word, yet unlike any other of his class."*

AND WHILE MOST OF HIS CONTEMPORARIES were dressed in keeping with the terrain over which they operated, Wild Bill Hickok blended "the immaculate neatness of the dandy with the extravagant taste and style of the frontiersman," which befitted the man Custer regarded as "the most famous scout of the Plains."

James Butler "Wild Bill" Hickok

Even when divested of his plainsman's furs and buckskins, Hickok's garb remained dandified: colored vests or waistcoats, fashionable jackets with broad lapels and boiled white shirts with cravat or tie; his high-heeled boots were worn with the tops inside his trousers; the whole was surmounted by a broad-brimmed, flat-crowned, white or black sombrero-type hat. In his later years, Hickok also sported a fashionable cane. At such times, of course, his pistols were tactfully kept out of sight. However, when employed in peacekeeping duties in places such as Hays City or Abilene, his dandified image gave way to more practical dress and, during the summer months, he was often seen wandering around in shirtsleeves with his two holstered Colt Navy pistols, butts forward, prominently displayed.

Hickok's physical appearance and bearing were eagerly seized upon in Col. George Ward Nichols' article published in the February 1867 *Harper's New Monthly Magazine* and by the Welsh-born Henry M. Stanley (who, in a couple of years, would immortalize himself with the greeting, "Dr. Livingstone, I presume?"). Photographic and written descriptions of Hickok indicate that he stood over six feet tall, was broad shouldered, narrow waisted and wore his auburn hair shoulder length in the manner of the plainsmen. Curiously, his moustache was straw-colored; its length dictated by fashion. His features, too, were distinctive: a broad forehead, high cheekbones, aquiline nose, strong chin and long jawbones; all dominated by a pair of blue-gray eyes that in normal discourse were benign and friendly, though when he was aroused by danger became coldly implacable.

Hickok's reputation as a gunfighter naturally included his ability to get a pistol into action "as quick as thought," but in reality, speed was probably the last thing on his mind. Hickok told Col. Nichols that one should take time and not be hurried, which meant that reaction to a situation counted far more than speed—when Hickok went for his pistols, he had already anticipated the outcome.

If we ignore Hickok's leg-pulling, his elevation from noted scout and plainsman to the most notorious man-killer on the border remains a mystery. A cursory examination discloses that he did not deserve such a reputation. Between 1861–71—the period that covers his pistol-wielding ventures—there are only seven authenticated killings involving Hickok. He may (or may not) have shot David C. McCanles at Rock Creek, Nebraska, in July 1861, yet it wasn't until four years later, in July 1865, that he shot it out with Dave Tutt in Springfield, Missouri. There was then another gap until August 1869, when as acting sheriff of Ellis

Whereas Buffalo Bill Cody was drawn to the stage, Wild Bill Hickok (above and second from left in group photo) quickly realized that it was not for him and, following a number of disputes with his costars over his stage pranks, he quit in March 1874. Hickok returned West, accompanied by $1,000 and a pair of .44 caliber Smith & Wesson "American" revolvers presented to him by Cody and partner Texas Jack Omohundro as parting gifts.

HICKOK'S ADVENTURES

By 1872, Hickok had abandoned both the Plains and his stints as a peace officer, and instead took up gambling as a profession and a pastime. He also engaged in other pursuits, among them acting as a guide for tourists or hunters and, in an historic appearance at Niagara Falls, he was a master of ceremonies for the "Grand Buffalo Hunt." This was a financial disaster, but the public's reaction to Hickok probably influenced him when he accepted an offer from Cody to join his theatrical *Combination* a year later. One suspects that the large salary tempted Hickok rather than the publicity involved. When Ned Buntline had approached him to write up his adventures, Hickok reportedly refused to speak to him. Buntline turned to Cody as a source, but when Buntline and Cody ended their partnership because of a disagreement over profits, Cody persuaded Hickok to join him and Omohundro on the stage.

When scouting for George Armstrong Custer, Hickok did not ride a prancing mare called Black Nell. Instead, he rode a fine Army mule.

County, Kansas, he shot and killed Bill Mulvey (or Mulrey) and then Samuel Strawhun in September. Ten months later in July 1870, again in Hays, Kansas, he shot two Seventh Cavalry troopers in a saloon brawl, killing one and wounding the other. And finally, in October 1871 in Abilene, when attempting to deal with a large band of drunken Texas cowboys, he shot Phil Coe and also his own friend Mike Williams who had stepped into the line of fire—a far cry from the "considerably over a hundred" so-called bad men Hickok is said to have killed.

In hindsight, however, it is understandable why such outrageous stories were not denied, especially when Hickok himself rarely gave interviews. Few people got to know the real man or any facts about him, and it is only by examining comments from those who actually knew Hickok, and his own rare letters to the press, that we can get some idea of his true character. From these excursions, we learn that he enjoyed books, feminine company, good conversation and socializing. He also displayed a good knowledge of the West, and he was considered an expert on the guerrilla warfare that had pervaded parts of Kansas, Missouri and Arkansas during the Civil War.

Following his appearance in *Harper's*, Hickok, along with a number of other plainsmen, was hired to scout for the Seventh Cavalry. He was sent into action against hostile Indians in Kansas in the spring and summer of 1867. Hickok soon achieved a reputation as an Indian scout, but unlike his myth, he did not ride a prancing mare called Black Nell. Instead, he rode a fine Army mule, which was better than a horse when riding over rough country. Some even

Hickok's taste in dandified clothing can be seen in this photograph, hardly the image of a ruthless gunfighter.

thought mules to be the equal of the fleet Indian ponies. Indeed, on one occasion when he ran out of supplies, Lt. Col. George Armstrong Custer ordered Hickok to ride by night on a fresh mule to request supply wagons be sent to his command.

Between military engagements, Hickok served as a deputy U.S. marshal in Kansas, and in 1869 he was elected acting sheriff of Ellis County, making Hays City his headquarters. Later, in 1871, he was appointed marshal of Abilene during its last season as a cowtown. Hickok was not a professional peace officer, but took the job seriously, and some described him as a "terror to evil-doers."

Wild Bill Hickok is one of America's foremost frontier folk heroes, but the real man remains controversial. To some he was heroic, and to others, an overbearing bully, a braggart and by others, he was called a coward—but never to his face. In contradiction to the latter opinion stands the trust placed in him by various army officers, two U.S. marshals and the people who employed him as a lawman. Make no mistake, Hickok had his faults, but he was also a man of character, integrity, courage and action. For that, he deserves his reputation.

Hickok was still in Springfield, Missouri, when, in February 1873, it was reported that he had been murdered by Texans at Kansas' Fort Dodge. A number of sympathetic obituaries appeared before Hickok himself announced that reports of his death were premature, but for the benefit of the Kansas City papers he declared: "I am dead!" He also seized the opportunity to take a swipe at Ned Buntline, whose abortive attempts to kill him off with his pen had failed, and "having failed, he is now, so I am told, trying to have it done by some Texans, but he has signally failed so far."

Back in Kansas City in the summer of 1874, Hickok resumed his gambling and occasional ventures as a scout and guide for hunters and tourists. Later, he moved to Cheyenne, Wyoming, and, over the following 18 months, also spent time in St. Louis, Missouri. On March 5, 1876, he married Agnes Lake Thatcher in Cheyenne. They had first met in 1871 when he was marshal of Abilene and her circus played in town. They kept in touch by mail, and their decision to marry was welcomed by Hickok's friends and the local press. After a short honeymoon, Hickok left Agnes in Cincinnati with relatives and returned West, promising to send for her when he was settled. Unfortunately, they never met again, for Hickok met his untimely death at the hands of back-shooting Jack McCall on the afternoon of Wednesday, August 2, 1876.

It will always be, however, his real and imaginary skill with a pistol and his disputed man-killing reputation that will be best remembered. That he was an excellent pistol shot is no longer in doubt, though one could be forgiven for doubting some of the "miraculous" feats that defy man and weapon. Yet, they form a part of the legend of a man who, despite his faults and weaknesses, stood head and shoulders above many of his contemporaries, and displayed a strength of character that set him apart. Many men swore to kill him, some with a real or imagined grievance, and others seeking a cheap reputation as his killer. Few of them would dare meet him face-to-face. While they are now obscure and long forgotten, Wild Bill Hickok in all his guises, as both hero and a frontier icon, remains.

FROM TROY GROVE TO THE TIN STAR

WILD BILL HICKOK EARNED HIS LAWMAN STRIPES

LONG *before he became acting sheriff of Ellis County, Kansas, and later marshal of Abilene, Kansas, James Butler Hickok had served in several law enforcement capacities.*

Wild Bill Hickok, far left in white hat, was a deputy U.S. marshal when this photograph was taken by Alexander Gardner at Kansas' Fort Harker, circa September 1867.

HIS FIRST APPOINTMENT WAS AS ONE of four constables elected early in 1858 by the citizens of Monticello, Johnson County, Kansas. He was to serve the local magistrates. Then came the Civil War.

William Hickok, as he was known to most of his companions during the war—before the more familiar Wild Bill earned him notoriety in Southwest Missouri and parts of Arkansas—rendered signal service to the Union. In fact, Gen. John B. Sanborn, who commanded the District of Southwest Missouri, later declared that Hickok was the best and coolest scout he had.

Colonel George Ward Nichols' article on "Wild Bill," published in *Harper's New Monthly Magazine* in February 1867, contained some fiction, but it did describe several of Hickok's real activities behind enemy lines, and it prompted editorial comment in a number of Kansas and Missouri newspapers, together with statements from those who knew the real Hickok. For the historian, however, unraveling fact from fiction is a task far from finished; yet, one thing is certain—Hickok was a resourceful individual who got himself out of a number of hazardous situations during and following the conflict.

Hickok first entered government service as a wagonmaster in the fall of 1861 and served until September 1862. There is then a gap until early 1864, when he is listed as a provost marshal's police detective. It is this missing period that is of most concern, for it covers the time when, according to *Harper's*, he scouted for Gen. Samuel R. Curtis in Arkansas. Perhaps he did (that claim is still under investigation); but recent research, backtracking from 1864,

Deputy U.S. Marshal James Butler Hickok in 1867, photo taken in Leavenworth, Kansas. Note the ornate watch fob and chain.

reveals that his employment by the provost marshal in Springfield probably began sometime in 1863. In this capacity, Hickok carried out some bizarre tasks, which included visiting saloons to check on the number of soldiers drinking when they should have been on duty; or investigating the activities of known liquor dealers who did not have a license.

On occasion, "William" Hickok (curiously, no one seems to have questioned the fact that he signed himself J.B. Hickok on official documents) was also sent into parts of Missouri and Arkansas, under secret orders, in pursuit of wanted individuals. One time, Detective Hickok was sent into a Missouri township near Springfield to obtain $1,000 in cash from a wanted individual and two of his companions. Hickok was also to make an inventory of their property to that amount. Not surprisingly, Hickok reported that nothing was achieved as all three men had disappeared.

This tintype of Hickok was made circa 1863. In 1864, he was employed as a special policeman, and later he was attached to Brig. Gen. John B. Sanborn's headquarters in Springfield, Missouri.

By April 1864, Hickok had had enough of chasing shadows and miscreant soldiery, and on April 2, at his own request, he was transferred to the quartermaster and reengaged as a scout. In June, Sanborn enlisted him. Hickok was paid five dollars a day and supplied with a horse and equipment, which presumably included firearms. From then on, the "Wild Bill" of *Harper's* and the real Hickok blended in this period of scouting and spying that has become legendary.

Wild Bill Hickok (left)—pictured here with John Burwell "Texas Jack" Omohundro (center) and Buffalo Bill Cody, circa 1873—tried performing in Buffalo Bill's Wild West Show but didn't like it.

Following the end of the war and the much publicized shoot-out in Springfield, Missouri, with his erstwhile friend Davis K. Tutt on July 21, 1865, Hickok was at a loose end. Late in January 1866, however, his old quartermaster, Capt. Richard Bentley Owen (immortalized in *Harper's* as "Captain Honesty"), was transferred from Springfield to become quartermaster in Fort Riley, Kansas. He sent for Hickok and appointed him government detective to "hunt up public property," for which he was paid the princely sum of $125 a month (later reduced to $75). In this capacity, Hickok tracked down deserters and others who had "misappropriated" government mules and horses. Hickok proved his worth.

In May, Hickok was detached from the post to guide Gen. William T. Sherman and party to Fort Kearny, Nebraska. (Oddly, in the 1880s, Sherman will write to Buffalo Bill Cody, reflecting upon the trip and his admiration for him. Cody promptly published the letter in his show programs, though he was well aware that Sherman had gotten his "Bills" mixed up, for in May 1866, Cody was still in Leavenworth, Kansas.) At Fort Kearny, Gen. John S. Pope then engaged Hickok as his guide to Santa Fe. Hickok returned to Fort Riley in September.

General Winfield Hancock's Kansas campaign against hostile Indians in early 1867 led to Hickok being transferred from detective work to scouting for Lt. Col. George Armstrong Custer's Seventh Cavalry. He served Custer until July 31 when hostilities ceased. Within weeks, it was reported that he had been appointed as a deputy U.S. marshal.

Some have claimed that Hickok was appointed deputy U.S. marshal at Fort Riley as early as 1866, but no documentary proof has been found. Rather, available records unearthed in Washington, D.C., indicate that Charles C. Whiting, the newly appointed U.S. marshal for the District of Kansas, appointed Hickok to deputy in August 1867.

According to official records (there are some gaps), Hickok served intermittently as a deputy between 1867–70 and earned in excess of $1,000 in fees and expenses. He was now involved in federal rather than civil cases. These included desertions from the army, horse and mule thefts, illicit liquor sales and counterfeiting U.S. currency. The earliest case found to date involving Hickok was in October 1867 when he arrested James Quinlin, who had been subpoenaed to appear in Topeka, Kansas, in the case of the United States vs. John Reynard on a charge of counterfeiting.

Late in 1867, Deputy U.S. Marshal B. Searcy and Hickok were featured in an amusing commentary in the short-lived *Ellsworth Tri-Weekly Advertiser* after Hickok's arrest of John Hurst, which resulted in Marshal Whiting and Searcy being called in to testify as witnesses. In the first issue, dated December 25, the editor remarked that when he came to move his printing press into the new office, he needed some assistance, and Hickok and "Captain Searcy" offered to help. "If some of our printer friends had seen Wild Bill take hold of the heavy fly-wheel of our Wells' Power Press and lift it over the stair step bannister—two and a half feet high—they would exclaim appropriately and westernly, 'bully for Bill.'"

Hired to hunt down counterfeiters, Wild Bill Hickok became a victim himself in 1870 when someone passed him bogus money at a Missouri race track.

Counterfeiting was a lucrative pastime, and in 1870, Hickok himself was a victim. In Junction City, he roomed with James Atkinson, who blithely informed Hickok that he was passing dud money, but if it was recognized, he took it back. Hickok was not impressed. One such note was later circulated at a race track in Missouri and passed to Hickok, who was furious. His inquiries led to Atkinson, and he immediately filed a complaint and swore out a warrant. Learning that Atkinson had fled to Abilene, Hickok set off in pursuit. It is likely that he enlisted the aid of Abilene's marshal, Thomas J. "Bear River" Smith, in locating his quarry. (Smith was murdered in November which, ironically, paved the way for Hickok's own appointment as marshal of Abilene in April 1871.) However, when counterfeiter Atkinson finally came to trial in October, the case was not fully prosecuted; he escaped imprisonment and doubtless made himself scarce.

During 1868–70, Hickok was involved in several horse and mule theft cases. In March 1868, when Marshal Whiting learned that the army had some alleged horse thieves in custody at Kansas' Fort Hays, he wrote to the commanding officer on

March 19 and requested that he "notify Mr. J.B. Hickok at Hays City who will promptly respond to your notice." Nine days later, Hickok wrote to the post commander, requesting a guard to help him convey his prisoners to Topeka. Accompanying Hickok on this occasion was his longtime friend William F. Cody, not yet generally known as Buffalo Bill. Cody was a government detective who had been ordered in pursuit of a gang of thieves—some were thought to be the men in custody at Fort Hays. Hickok, Cody and a military escort delivered the men safely to jail in Topeka, where they eventually went on trial.

In May 1869, shortly after returning from a visit to his mother's home in Illinois, Hickok was ordered to Kansas' Fort Wallace to escort two alleged horse thieves and two witnesses to Topeka. The men, Silas Baker and Willard Curtis, were later sentenced to four and a half years in the state penitentiary.

In Topeka, however, Hickok learned that an incident in Ellsworth, Kansas, that had occurred in March threatened his future as a deputy U. S. marshal. A number of Pawnee Indians had been killed by local residents who feared that they would go on the rampage. Three of those alleged to be involved were Deputy U. S. Marshals John S. Park, Chauncey B. Whitney and B. Searcy (sometimes spelled Circey). The deputies had tried to ease the situation and arrest the Indians for their own protection, but the subsequent shooting led to Marshal Whiting being called to account for their actions. In defense of his deputies, he described Park and Whitney as good men but, for a reason not disclosed, said that Searcy was not in his employ and that he was a "man of bad character. One of the worst, in fact, to be found on the Western border of Kansas."

The ax fell, and on May 19, Whiting was dismissed. In the months that followed, his health deteriorated, and on January 2, 1870, he died, a much maligned and mourned individual. In his place, however, the government appointed Dana W. Houston who made it his first task to interview all of Whiting's deputies and many of those appointed by the district court. Many were fired, but Hickok was among those Houston retained.

Between his duties as the acting sheriff of Ellis County, Kansas, in the fall of 1869, Hickok continued to act as a deputy U. S. marshal. In November, he obtained a warrant for the arrest of illegal timber cutters reported to be at work on Paradise Creek, some miles from Fossil Creek Station (present-day Russell, Kansas). Arriving by train, Hickok hired a horse and set out. Years later, Adolph Roenigk recalled that when Hickok stepped off the train, he "wore a broad-brimmed hat and a brand new buckskin suit with fringes on his elbow sleeves and trouser legs. A pair of six-shooters strapped to his sides, he made the appearance of just such a picture as one could see on the cover of a dime novel." With the help of First Lt. L.W. Cooke of the Third Infantry, Hickok arrested John Hobbs, Charles Hamilton and Charles Vernon, who were taken to Topeka. The outcome of the trial, or whether one actually took place, is not known, though Hobbs became well-known in Hays City in the late 1870s.

Time will doubtless disclose more information on Hickok's services in law enforcement, but from what we have learned so far, there is little doubt that he was indeed a useful and reliable individual in whatever capacity he was called upon to act.

ORLANDO "RUBE" ROBBINS

IDAHO'S FEARLESS LAWMAN

ASK *most Americans to name a few intrepid lawmen from the 19th century, and they are almost certain to list Wild Bill Hickok, Bat Masterson and Wyatt Earp.*

THESE HEROES OF YESTERYEAR epitomize the bold lawmen who tamed the frontier with their six-guns and tin stars. For nearly a century, Hollywood has immortalized these valiant peacekeepers, embellishing their reputations until it is often difficult to separate fact from fantasy.

Query other Americans about which Western town was the most lawless, and they're apt to say Dodge City, Tombstone or Deadwood. Thanks to the movies and the dime novels before them, the mention of these old cow and mining towns brings to mind images of gunslingers, drunken cowboys, gamblers and a gutsy sheriff or marshal who brought them to heel.

Yet, there were more wild towns and daring lawmen than those that are most often brought to mind.

In the second half of the nineteenth century, the Idaho Territory had its share of rowdy towns. The mining centers of Idaho City and Silver City competed with Deadwood and Tombstone, not only for the amount of rich ore their citizens produced, but also for the number of hard men they attracted. While Wyatt Earp and his brothers held sway in the Arizona desert, an equally fearless lawman faced down desperados in Idaho. His name was Orlando "Rube" Robbins.

Robbins was born in Maine on August 30, 1836. When he was a teenager, he acquired

Many of the outlaws apprehended by "Rube" Robbins served time in the Old Idaho State Penitentiary in Boise.

a yoke of oxen, which he valued highly. He used the oxen on his family's farm and occasionally earned money by hiring them out to neighbors. When Robbins was 17 years old, his father sold the oxen without asking his son for permission. Raging with anger, the young man bid his father good riddance and left home for good.

Any criminal having Robbins on his trail might as well consider himself already behind bars.

Robbins eventually found his way to the California mining camps in the foothills of the Sierra Nevada Mountains. When he was 25, gold strikes along Idaho's Clearwater River and in Florence Basin (a few miles northeast of Riggins, Idaho) lured him away from California. Two years later, in August 1863, he relocated again, drifting south to the new diggings in Boise Basin (about 20 miles northeast of modern-day Boise).

A year old at the time Robbins arrived, the Boise Basin gold rush was producing the largest stampede of miners and hangers-on since the heyday of California's Mother Lode. Numerous mining camps—they quickly grew into small cities—dotted the landscape, sporting names such as Placerville, Centerville and West Bannack. Robbins gravitated to West Bannack, which was the fastest growing of the towns with over 6,100 people. Wanting a name that fit West Bannack's prominence as the largest settlement in the Pacific Northwest, the Territorial Legislature soon rechristened it Idaho City.

At the time Robbins moved to the boomtown, it boasted a hospital, a theater, two bowling alleys, four sawmills, a mattress factory, nine restaurants, two churches, four breweries and 25 saloons, all opened within the first 12 months of its founding. The town also had 15 doctors and more than two dozen lawyers. But what Idaho City needed more than a horde of sawbones and shysters was law and order. And it found it in Rube Robbins. In 1864, he became deputy sheriff.

With the Civil War raging in the East, the Boise Basin miners polarized around the Union and Confederate causes. Fueled by whiskey, Northern and Southern sympathizers often bloodied one another with fists, knives and sometimes guns as they used force to show their opinions. Many an evening, Robbins had to lock up a drunken loudmouth who was threatening to punch or shoot to demonstrate his political beliefs to an equally intoxicated opponent (who was just as certain that God was on his side).

Early one July, the town's Southern contingent vowed that it would not allow any Yankee to sing the "Star Spangled Banner" on Independence Day. Learning of the bluster, Robbins became infuriated. He was for the Union, and no mob of Rebel-leaning rabble was going to curtail his free speech.

On July 4, he stepped into a barroom overflowing with Southerners. Ignoring the drunken toasts to Jefferson Davis and the Confederate cause, he walked over to a billiard table, climbed atop its green felt and pulled his revolvers. As everyone stared at the two cap-and-ball pistols, the saloon fell as quiet as a prayer meeting.

"Oh, say can you see by the dawn's ear-ly light, . . ." the deputy's baritone voice boomed out the song's three-quarter time.

"What so proud-ly we hail'd at the twilight's last gleam-ing. . . ?" Robbins watched the crowd as he sang, but no one so much as twitched an eyelash.

"O'er the land of the free and the home of the brave?"

With his eyes still locked on the crowd, Robbins holstered his guns and hopped off the table. In place of his singing, a ponderous silence filled the barroom. Pushing his way through a sea of glares, the lawman walked to the front door and onto the street. Not one Southerner made a move to stop him.

Robbins and Egan fired lead with as much abandon as their medieval counterparts had swung sword and mace.

Robbins' reputation soon earned him a job in Boise, where he served first as a deputy sheriff and then as a U.S. marshal.

In late February 1868, miners working the Golden Chariot Mine beneath Silver City—a boomtown located in the Owyhee Mountains about 60 miles southwest of Boise—burrowed into a shaft belonging to the Ida Elmore Mine. For several weeks, the two factions cussed and fumed, each side accusing the other of tunneling beyond its claim.

On March 25, tensions came to a head when a party of armed Golden Chariot miners invaded the Ida Elmore shaft. A subterranean gunfight soon erupted and then escalated until 100 men were engaged in the battle, which was known as the Owyhee War. For three days, the two underground armies fired at each other, spraying so much lead into the Ida Elmore's support timbers that the mine nearly collapsed.

When news of the war reached Idaho's territorial governor, he issued an order demanding that the two sides immediately end their fighting and settle their feud in court. The job of delivering the governor's proclamation and forcing a truce was given to Robbins.

Averaging an amazingly fast 10 miles per hour over roads that were mud-cloaked by the spring rains and mountain snowmelt, the lone deputy rode from Boise to Silver City in six hours. Soon after arriving, Robbins brought the heads of the warring parties together and read the governor's edict. No doubt he also informed them that he would personally ensure that the proclamation was obeyed. Knowing his reputation, the Golden Chariot and Ida Elmore owners took the deputy at his word. After calling off their gunmen, the adversaries drew up new boundaries for their mines and never needed to go to court. Robbins had settled the entire affair in a single day.

Facing down drunks and arbitrating disputes were not the only things at which the deputy excelled. He also knew how to catch criminals. In February 1876, after six bandits held up the Silver City stage as it neared Boise, Robbins had them locked up in jail within two days of the robbery.

In addition to his duties in law enforcement, Robbins also held the rank of colonel in the territorial militia and was head of scouts. During Idaho's Camas War in the late 1870s, he and his command were part of a larger U.S. Army force that pursued a band of Bannock and Paiute Indians, led by a Paiute war chief named Egan, into the Owyhee badlands southwest of Silver City (near the Idaho-Oregon border). For nearly two weeks, the army chased the hostiles across the high desert, some days riding 50 miles.

In late June 1878, as was later recounted by a militia eyewitness, Col. Robbins and four of his troops were riding over a ridge when they were jumped by a party of Bannocks that included Chief Egan. Outnumbered by the warriors, the scouts spurred their horses to a gallop, trying to reach the army lines. The Indians pressed the pursuit, firing as they rode. Just when it appeared the militiamen would keep their scalps, the Bannocks wounded a scout named Bill Myers and killed his horse. Hearing Myers' cry for help, Robbins wheeled about to go to his rescue.

While Robbins raced toward the fallen trooper, Chief Egan whipped more speed out of his horse in order to cut between them. As the famed lawman and Indian leader drew closer together, they finally recognized one another. Their warrior spirits inflamed, the two combatants charged each other with their Winchesters blazing. Acting like Knights of the Round Table on a battleground in the Middle Ages, Robbins and Egan fired lead with as much abandon as their medieval counterparts had swung sword and mace.

Their rifles empty, the chief and Indian fighter drew their pistols. Sitting atop his dancing steed, Robbins blasted away with his revolvers, impervious to the lead that tore through his clothes and nicked his finger. Chief Egan also showed his mettle, deftly using his horse for cover as he dodged Robbins' bullets. And then one of the lawman's shots found its mark, hitting Egan in the wrist and knocking him off his mount. Quickly regaining his senses, the chief scrambled to his feet, ready for a fight to the death. But before Robbins could renew his aim, trooper Myers raised his gun and shot Egan in the chest.

Siver City, Idaho, no doubt looked more "modern" when this photo was taken in the 1890s than it did in 1868 when Orlando "Rube" Robbins quelled an underground mining battle.

Leaving the gravely wounded chief to his tribesmen, Robbins helped Myers up behind his saddle and escaped.

Just like Hickok, Masterson and the Earp brothers . . .

Seven weeks later, Robbins again demonstrated his cool head. He was crossing the Snake River in a rowboat with an army lieutenant named W.R. Parnell, a bugler and two cavalrymen when a horse they had tethered to their boat panicked. As the soldiers tried to free the animal, it bumped their boat, spilling everyone into the water. While Lt. Parnell and the bugler began drifting with the current, Robbins helped one of the cavalrymen climb onto the overturned hull. The other cavalryman caught the horse's tail and hung on as it swam to shore.

Seeing the bugler start to founder, Robbins abandoned the safety of the rowboat and went to his aid. No sooner had he maneuvered the bugler into the shallows than Robbins noticed the lieutenant was beginning to tire. Once more, he dove into the river, reaching Parnell as he was about to go under. Robbins kept the sputtering officer afloat until another boat came to their rescue.

During the 1880s and 1890s, Robbins continued to pursue desperadoes across Southern Idaho. In August 1882, shortly before his 46th birthday, he arrested the outlaw Charley Chambers after covering 1,280 miles in just 13 days. Any criminal having Robbins on his trail might as well consider himself already behind bars.

Unlike many lawmen of his day, Robbins had a life apart from gunplay and daring. When he was in his thirties, he became a Christian and joined the temperance movement. Following his baptism in the Boise River, he was elected president of the Methodist Church Sunday School. He also served a term in the Idaho Territorial Legislature, and some years later, he gained appointment as its sergeant at arms.

When Robbins was in his late sixties, he transported prisoners for the Idaho State Penitentiary. Although he escorted men who were often one-third his age, he never allowed any of them to get away.

Idaho's most famous lawman died of a heart attack on May 1, 1908. During his funeral, numerous dignitaries paid him homage, each attempting to take his measure. But none of these orations came close to the tribute spoken years earlier by the outlaw Cherokee Bob.

As he lay bleeding to death from Robbins' gunshot, the bandit said the marshal never jumped to the side after shooting, but "always sprang through the smoke [of his revolver] and advanced upon his opponent, firing as he came."

Just like Hickok, Masterson and the Earp brothers, Orlando "Rube" Robbins was a paladin of the Old West and a credit and an honor to all Americans "in the land of the free and the home of the brave."

THE SPLIT

DID DOC & WYATT SPLIT BECAUSE OF A RACIAL SLUR?

ALMOST *five years had passed since the gas-lit world of saloons and gambling halls brought Wyatt Earp and Doc Holliday together in Texas.*

THEY APPEAR TO HAVE ENJOYED each other's company from the outset, but on the night of September 19, 1878, in Dodge City, Kansas, the bond between them was sealed when Doc saved Wyatt's life in "a scrimmage" with Texas drovers that left one man with a bandaged head and a soldier shot in the leg.

Wyatt's gratitude for that night's work explains much about his friendship with the well-educated but sometimes hot-headed and troublesome Georgian.

For his part, backing the Earp brothers' play became Doc's habit in Tombstone, even before the October 26, 1881, street fight. He and Wyatt did have things in common: both

Front Street in Dodge City, Kansas, circa 1879, less than a year after Doc Holliday waded into a scrape with Texas drovers, saving Wyatt Earp's life.

were gamblers, both fastidious dressers, both men who lived by their wits and their guns, but Doc was the son of good family whose ambitions were thwarted by disease, while Wyatt was a would-be entrepreneur determined to improve his lot in the world. Doc fed Wyatt's need for wit, intelligent conversation and culture, while Wyatt and his brothers provided Doc with a sense of family and purpose. But the core of their friendship was an absolute and mutual conviction that they could count on one another no matter what.

Wyatt was upset that Doc and the other posse members took cover when the shooting began

In July 2001, coauthor Chuck Hornung was in New Mexico, researching his book on the New Mexico Mounted Police. One Sunday, he decided to take a break from his labors and join his brother-in-law at Albuquerque's big weekend flea market. While there, he found a copy of Miguel A. Otero, Jr.'s *My Nine Years as Governor of the Territory of New Mexico, 1897-1906* (1940) at the bargain price of $7.50. Later, as he was examining his prize, he found in its pages the folded carbon copy of an undated, unsigned letter filled with potentially explosive new data on the Earp vendetta posse of 1882.

First, the most arresting find in this letter has been the subject of controversy and speculation for decades. Shortly after Wyatt Earp and Doc Holliday arrived in Albuquerque, New Mexico, in April 1882, a four-year period in which they had been extremely close came to an abrupt end. In May 1882, newspapers reported that Wyatt and Doc had quarreled in Albuquerque and that Doc and Dan Tipton had left the rest of the posse and proceeded to Trinidad, Colorado. What was the quarrel about? One tale, almost absurd, was told that the two men argued because Wyatt had worn a steel vest at the Iron Springs fight with Curly Bill Brocius, and that Doc thought Wyatt should take the same chances as everyone else. A second hypothesis also had to do with the Iron Springs fight. In this explanation, Wyatt was upset that Doc and the other posse members took cover when the shooting began, leaving Wyatt exposed and fighting alone. A third, more general theory was that Doc got drunk and talked too freely about the events that had recently transpired in Arizona. This letter may finally put the question to rest.

Another important issue brought to light is the extent to which the Earps and Doc had the support not only of local mining and business interests in Tombstone, but also of corporate interests, including Wells Fargo and the Santa Fe Railroad. Wells Fargo made an unprecedented public endorsement of the Earps on March 23, 1882, and rumors would later name Wells Fargo as a player in thwarting the extradition of Doc back to Arizona from Colorado to stand trial for the murder of Frank Stilwell. Denver newspapers speculated that powerful forces were at work to prevent Doc's forced return to Arizona Territory. Who were these forces, and how far did their influence reach?

The recently discovered letter throws light on both of these questions and more. It follows here in full.

DEAR OLD FRIEND,

It was good to hear from you and to learn all is well in Albuquerque. Yes, I knew Wyatt Earp. I knew him to be a gentleman and he held a reputation of being an excellent law officer. I knew the Earp brothers first in Kansas, but did not [see] much [of] them after that time. My father knew them best. I knew Doc Holliday at Las Vegas and told that adventure in My Life on the Frontier [Vol.] I.

*I tired [tried] to help them in their quest to stay in New Mexico following the Tombstone trouble. The Lake book you mentioned [*Wyatt Earp: Frontier Marshal*] did not relate the matter, Earp and Holliday and some others stayed in Albuquerque a couple of weeks while [New Mexico Gov. Lionel A.] Sheldon and the powers of the Santa Fe [Railroad] and Wells Fargo tried to work out some kind of arrangement.*

Earp [Wyatt] stayed at Jaffa's home and the other boys were around town. Jaffa gave Earp an overcoat from his store, Earp's had been ruined in a fight with the Cow-boys. I remember that cold wind even today. I do not remember that the boys had much money.

Father sent me to see to the comfort of the Earp posse because his railroad supported the boys. Earp had a long meeting with the president of Wells Fargo, but I can not say about the direction of the talk.

One afternoon I drove Earp and Jaffa to the river to see them building the new bridge. Earp remarked how it reminded him of the big bridge at Wichita. Some days later, Earp and Holliday had a falling out at Fat Charlie's [proprietor of the Retreat Restaurant in Albuquerque] one night. They were eating when Holliday said something about Earp being a Jew boy. Something like Wyatt are you becoming a damn Jew boy? Earp became angry and left. Charlie said that Holliday knew he had said it wrong, he never saw them together again. Jaffa told me later that Earp's woman was a Jewess. Earp did mu-- [illegible/mezuzah?] when entering his house.

Wells Fargo arranged safety in Colorado and the road gave them passage to Trinidad. I remember that Blonger and Armijo kept watch over the boys. I was able later, when governor, to reward Armijo for that favor to my father. That is all I know about the Earps.

My health is not good at present. I spend much time confined to my bed. I am glad you found my new book of interest. My best to the Mrs. and season's greetings to all.

Yours sincerely yours,

The internal evidence of the letter clearly identifies the writer as Miguel A. ("Gillie") Otero, Jr., former governor of New Mexico Territory and the author of four books, including the two which are mentioned in the body of the text, volume one of *My Life on the Frontier, 1864–1882* (1935) and *My Nine Years as Governor of New Mexico, 1897–1906* (1940). As Otero refers to the latter as "my new book" and mentions "season's greetings," the letter may reasonably be assumed to have been written in December 1940. This conclusion is supported by a second Otero letter that mentions Wyatt Earp, this one written to Watson Reed, August 17, 1940 (located by Old West historian Allen Barra in 1998), which appears to have been typed on the same typewriter. Furthermore, the Albuquerque newspapers in 1882 confirm that Otero was in town while the Earp posse was there.

Though the primary focus of the letter is Otero's efforts to help the Earp party "stay in New Mexico," Otero's explanation of the quarrel that brought the dynamic Wyatt Earp/Doc Holliday duo to an end can't be ignored. Otero's comments regarding Henry Jaffa and Earp support his reason for the split—Jaffa was Jewish, and it appears from the letter that while staying in Jaffa's home, Wyatt honored Jewish tradition. That Jaffa was a Jew and Wyatt was staying with him while Doc and the others were living in less spacious quarters may have contributed to Doc's slur about Wyatt "becoming a damn Jew boy."

Of course, Otero's letter points to yet another issue which would explain why Wyatt took the remark so seriously. Jaffa told Otero that "Earp's woman was a Jewess." What makes this particularly compelling is the fact that the relationship between Wyatt and Josephine Sarah "Sadie" Marcus in Tombstone was virtually unknown in 1940 when the letter was written, which means that the story had to come from someone with inside knowledge. That the explanation came from Wyatt's host, who was himself a Jew, suggests that Wyatt discussed his relationship while at the Jaffa home.

Jaffa's statement also contradicts recent arguments that the relationship between Wyatt and Sadie probably did not become a full-fledged affair until after they had left Tombstone. Doc's comment could have been merely a crude joke, or it could mean that Doc did not approve of Sadie. Doc's relationship to Sadie is unclear, but while he was under arrest in Denver in May 1882, he said that Cochise County Sheriff John Behan hated him because of a quarrel in which Doc accused Behan of gambling with money Doc had given Behan's "woman." Why Doc would have given money to Josephine Marcus was never explained.

During the Gunfight near the O.K. Corral, Doc Holliday risked his life for Wyatt Earp and his brothers. Yet, six months later, a feud ripped their friendship asunder.

Another intriguing comment concerns Jaffa's replacing Wyatt's overcoat because his "had been ruined in a fight with the Cow-boys." This offers supporting evidence for Wyatt Earp's claims of killing Curly Bill at Iron Springs. It is also true that, as Otero recounts, the new bridge over the Rio Grande was being constructed at the time the Earp party was in Albuquerque. Construction had begun in 1881, and it was not finished until December 1882.

In addition to the Earp-Holliday split, a major find in this letter is confirmation of widespread support for the Earp party. Otero identifies the parties involved in this effort as Gov. Lionel A. Sheldon of New

Wells Fargo's support of the Earps never wavered.

Mexico Territory, the Achison, Topeka and Santa Fe Railroad, and Wells, Fargo & Co. Young Otero was working on behalf of his father, Don Miguel Antonio Otero, merchant, banker and member of the board of directors and vice president of the Santa Fe Railroad. Otero says further that Wyatt "had a long meeting" with John J. Valentine, general superintendent of Wells Fargo in Albuquerque. He concludes that Wells Fargo "arranged safety in Colorado" for the Earps, and that the Santa Fe Railroad provided the posse men's passage to Trinidad and safety.

Can this letter's contents be supported by other evidence? First, it is obvious that powerful forces were at work on behalf of the Earps even before they left Arizona. In addition to the official color and support afforded by their status as deputy U.S. marshals, they received financial support from prominent Tombstone businessmen and members of the Citizens Safety Committee, as well as help from the big ranchers and Wells Fargo. After killing Curly Bill, the Earp party found refuge at Henry C. Hooker's Sierra Bonita ranch. While there, Dan Tipton brought them $1,000 from E.B. Gage, mining man and prominent vigilante; and Lou Cooley, a former stage driver who worked for Hooker and, at times, for Wells Fargo, delivered $1,000 from that company.

Stuart Lake (Wyatt biographer), John Flood, Jr. (Wyatt's secretary) and Forrestine Hooker (Henry's daughter-in-law) all claim in their writings that the Earps made one last visit to Tombstone for a meeting with the Citizens Committee. Hooker states that John N. Thacker of Wells Fargo was present. At that meeting, William Herring, attorney and spokesman for the vigilantes, advised Wyatt to leave Arizona until the furor died down and legal options could be weighed. Afterward, the Earps returned to Hooker's ranch and made a final sweep of the area, looking for cow-boys before they left the territory. They were aided and abetted by Col. James Biddle at Camp Grant, who allowed them to slip away although he knew them to be fugitives.

When Frederick W. Tritle arrived in Arizona Territory in early April 1882 to assume the governorship, he visited Tombstone, where he stayed with Milton Clapp, one of the leaders of the Citizens Safety Committee, and conferred with William Murray, Tritle's former business partner and another of the prominent vigilantes. As the *Tucson Citizen* reported, Tritle raised a posse to support Deputy U.S. Marshal John Henry Jackson (captain of the first company of Arizona Rangers) and wired President Chester A. Arthur about "the utter failure of the civil authority and the anarchy prevailing; the international trouble likely to grow out of this cattle thieving along the border, the fact that business is paralyzed and the fairest valleys in the Territory are kept from occupation by the presence of the Cow-boys."

Tritle would be the man who sent defective extradition papers to Colorado, seeking the return of Doc Holliday after his arrest in Denver in May 1882. Moreover, New Mexico Gov. Sheldon had a force in the field under Albert Jennings Fountain that was chasing after the cow-boys during the same period as the Earps' Vendetta Ride. Finally, Wells Fargo's support of the Earps never wavered. On April 14, 1882, Wells Fargo stage driver Lou Cooley met Wells Fargo General Superintendent John J. Valentine on the train in Benson. Afterward, Cooley was arrested in Willcox for "aiding and abetting the Earps."

It appears now, based on the Otero letter, that Valentine proceeded directly to his Albuquerque office after meeting Cooley. The *Albuquerque Evening Review* confirms Valentine was there on April 16 and 17. The Earps reached Silver City, New Mexico, on April 15, took the stage on April 16 to Deming, where they caught the train to Albuquerque, arriving that evening. Stuart Lake's notes at the Huntington Library say that Wyatt was met at the station by Frank McLain (McLean), later Wyatt's associate on the famous Dodge City Peace Commission, who took the Earps under his wing and later gave Wyatt $2,000. Whether this was a personal loan or McLain was acting on behalf of other individuals or organizations is not clear. In light of Otero's statement that he was sent to Albuquerque "to see to the comfort of the Earps," McLain may well have been his agent.

Remarkably, upon arrival in Albuquerque, Wyatt visited local newspapers and promised interviews provided that the papers would not report his presence until after he and his men had left town. Neither the *Morning Journal* or *Evening Review* mentioned that the Earps were in town until May 13, by which time the Earp brothers were in Gunnison, Colorado, and Doc Holliday was en route to Denver. The *Journal* did deny that it had interviewed Earp (the smaller Albuquerque newspapers have not been researched), but the Earps were known to be in town, which makes the silence nothing short of remarkable in light of the extent of press coverage on the Earp party's movements.

Otero's letter offers a clue to how that silence was accomplished. Jaffa, the businessman mentioned by Otero, was the president of New Albuquerque's Board of Trade, which acted as a quasi-government for the town. Sam Blonger, as marshal of "New Town," was appointed to that office by the sheriff of Bernalillo County, Perfecto Armijo, and approved by the Board of Trade. The town marshal's salary was paid by members of the Board of Trade, Jaffa's organization. Both Blonger and Armijo are mentioned by Otero as keeping watch "over the boys." Jaffa was a man who could make things happen.

The senior Otero's position with the Santa Fe Railroad lends further credence to the notion of brokered power on behalf of the Earps that eventually included the governors of Arizona Territory, New Mexico Territory and the state of Colorado. Otero specifically states that Wells Fargo arranged "safety in Colorado," and it is worth noting, in this respect, that Horace A.W. Tabor, mining magnate and lieutenant governor of Colorado, arrived in Las Vegas, New Mexico, the home of the ailing senior Otero, shortly after the Earps departed Albuquerque for Trinidad. Such a deal would also explain Doc's public remarks in Colorado that he had already been "pardoned" and his surprise when he was arrested in Denver. Further, it would explain the subsequent efforts brought to bear on Doc's behalf in Denver—which were so obvious, they caused press comment—and why the Earps were never arrested in Gunnison.

Of course, further research must be done, not only on the substance of the claims in the letter, but also on the provenance of the letter itself before final conclusions can be drawn. Preliminary research substantiates those aspects of the account relating to times, names and places that can be validated from the public record. If the letter holds up under further scrutiny, it confirms that the Earps had the support of powerful organizations and

The Earp party, sans Doc Holliday, landed in Gunnison, Colorado, after the events in Arizona and New Mexico. After the failed attempt to extradite Doc from Denver, Colorado, to Arizona, Doc joined Wyatt's group in Gunnison for a short time.

individuals on their Vendetta Ride. This support was sustained, in spite of the killings, and that eventually thwarted efforts to return them to Arizona. It also suggests that the Vendetta Ride was part of something much larger than the Earp-Clanton feud.

In light of other activities going on at the same time in both Arizona and New Mexico, such as Deputy U.S. Marshal Jackson's Ranger operations in Southern Arizona and New Mexico Volunteers Commander Fountain's search for cow-boys in New Mexico, as well as a presidential threat to use the army to restore order in Arizona Territory, the letter's revelations point to a determined federal effort supported (or perhaps instigated) by powerful economic interests (big ranchers, railroads, mining companies and Wells Fargo) and territorial authorities to suppress lawlessness in the Southwest.

On another level, the Otero letter provides circumstantial evidence supporting the description of the Iron Springs gunfight given by Wyatt, throws new light on the relationship between Wyatt and Sadie, and suggests that the reason the relationship between Wyatt and Doc cooled was much more personal than previously believed.

Taken together, if the revelations found in this letter hold up under further scrutiny, the letter will have to be considered a major find that fills in important pieces of the Tombstone puzzle. And note: you won't be the only one with an all-new interest in flea markets.

FIFTY THINGS YOU DON'T KNOW ABOUT WYATT EARP

THE TRUTH BEHIND THE LEGEND

EVERY *Old West history buff knows that Wyatt Earp took part in the gunfight near Tombstone, Arizona's O.K. Corral, but many of them are unaware that Wyatt was once arrested for stealing a horse. Here, then, are 50 facts about arguably the Old West's most famous lawman.*

1 ♦ Wyatt Earp was never a town marshal or a county sheriff. (He was the assistant marshal in Dodge City, Kansas, and a deputy U.S. marshal in Arizona.)

2 ♦ Wyatt's only known run for office was when he ran against and beat his half brother Newton for constable of Lamar, Missouri, in 1870.

3 ♦ There is no official record of Wyatt being legally married to two of his three wives. And two of Wyatt's so-called wives have been accused of being "on the line" (prostitutes).

4 ♦ Wyatt's full name was Wyatt Berry Stapp Earp, after his father's commanding officer in the Mexican War, Wyatt Berry Stapp.

5 ♦ It was snowing the day Wyatt was born.

6 ♦ Wyatt was sued three times for claim jumping in Eagle, Idaho.

7 ♦ Wyatt claimed in his autobiography that he used a telephone in Tombstone to call Benson. (Most researchers believe he wasn't recalling his time there correctly since Earp left Arizona by March 1882, and telephone lines from Tombstone to Benson weren't completed until years later.)

8 ♦ Wyatt liked to eat ice cream at Tombstone's Ice Cream Saloon on Fourth Street. (The Earps and Doc Holliday walked past it on their way to the fight near the O.K. Corral.)

9 ♦ There were five Earp brothers (not including their half brother Newton), who became known as "The Fighting Earps." Four were shot, and two died as a result. Their father Nicholas Earp was kicked by a mule. Only one Earp went through life without a scratch—Wyatt.

***Wyatt Earp often ate ice cream at the Ice Cream Saloon that advertised in the* Tombstone Nugget.**

10 ♦ Wyatt and two of his brothers, Morgan and Virgil, were often mistaken for one another. They were about six feet tall and weighed within three pounds of each other (at around 158 pounds).

11 ♦ Wyatt had no children—one of the few times in his life he shot blanks.

12 ♦ Wyatt was a longtime boxing devotee. In addition to the infamous bout he refereed in San Francisco (discussed later), he also refereed boxing matches in Tijuana, Mexico.

13 ♦ Wyatt was a bartender longer than he was a lawman.

14 ♦ Wyatt was accused of stealing schoolhouse funds (over $200) while acting as Lamar's constable.

15 ♦ Wyatt was arrested for stealing a horse in 1871.

16 ♦ Wyatt was incarcerated for horse stealing but escaped from jail and was never caught. Two other defendants in the horse-stealing affair were exonerated, or at least never convicted.

17 ♦ In 1872, Wyatt was arrested at least twice for consorting with prostitutes in Peoria, Illinois.

18 ♦ In 1874, several women named Earp were arrested for keeping a "bawdy house" in Wichita, Kansas. It is believed they were in the employ of some of the Earp men.

19 ♦ In 1876, while Wyatt was playing cards in a Wichita saloon, his revolver slipped from its holster and discharged as it hit the chair. The ball "passed through [Wyatt's] coat, struck the north wall then glanced off and passed through the ceiling," reported a local newspaper.

20 ♦ That same year, the Wichita city council accepted the police committee's recommendation, which stated that policemen Wyatt Earp and John Behrens had been collecting money in the town and had failed to turn it over to the city. Wyatt had already skipped town for Dodge City.

21 ♦ Wyatt made $75 a month as the assistant marshal of Dodge City, Kansas. (For comparison, a cow-boy usually made $30 a month and a soldier's monthly wages were $13.)

22 ♦ In the Spring of 1877, Wyatt hauled wood in Deadwood, Dakota Territory, and claimed to have made $130 a day in the process.

23 ♦ On the night of City Marshal Fred White's fatal shooting in Tombstone, Wyatt wasn't heeled (armed) and had to borrow a weapon. Thanks, in part, to Wyatt's testimony, bad man Curly Bill Brocius was exonerated for the killing.

24 ♦ Although lionized for single-handedly standing off a mob in the Johnny-Behind-the-Deuce affair, Wyatt isn't mentioned in any known newspaper accounts of the incident.

25 ♦ According to his sister-in-law Allie, Wyatt once hid in the kitchen to avoid buying raffle tickets he had promised a local school teacher, Miss Wynn.

26 ♦ The so-called Gunfight at the O.K. Corral didn't occur there. It took place in a vacant lot west of the rear entrance to the O.K. Corral. Why the bungled reference? See next entry.

27 ♦ Part of the reason the O.K. Corral has been mistakenly identified as the site of the famous Tombstone shoot-out is that Wyatt Earp made a map of the fight in 1926 and drew the fight's location in the wrong place (at the O.K. Corral's rear entrance).

Almost every day for a month, San Francisco newspapers ran articles about Earp refereeing the infamous Sharkey-Fitzsimmons fight after Earp announced, "Sharkey wins by a foul."

28 ♦ Wyatt didn't wear a holster at the famous fight. He testified at the subsequent hearing that he had pulled his pistol from his overcoat pocket.

29 ♦ The only persons not hit by gunfire in the O.K. gunfight were Ike Clanton (who ran away after the first salvo) and Wyatt Earp (who stayed until the bitter end).

30 ♦ Wyatt and Doc Holliday were jailed for over two weeks during the legal hearing about the gunfight. (Virgil and Morgan were exempted because of their wounds.)

31 ♦ After their 1882 so-called Vendetta Ride to avenge the death of Morgan Earp, Wyatt and Doc left Arizona as wanted men. They then had a falling out. One possible explanation is that a drunken Holliday complained about Wyatt's Jewish girlfriend, asking if Wyatt was becoming a "Jew boy."

32 ♦ Wyatt and his brother Virgil were pressured to resign their positions as deputy U.S. marshals because of criticism from the Tombstone townspeople that the Earp brothers were using their offices to persecute their personal enemies.

33 ♦ In 1885, Wyatt and two others were arrested for burglary in Hot Springs, Arkansas.

34 ♦ In 1888, Wyatt's second wife Mattie committed suicide. An acquaintance testified, after Mattie's overdose of laudanum, that Mattie had said Wyatt had wrecked her life by deserting her and she didn't want to live.

35 ♦ Wyatt was accused of throwing a prizefight in San Francisco. Acting as a last-minute replacement as referee, he called a foul on Bob Fitzsimmons (who was winning handily) and awarded the fight to Tom Sharkey (an upstart sailor). Fitzsimmons sued for the purse but lost on a technicality—prizefighting was illegal in San Francisco. Fitzsimmons fought in the ring for 34 years and lost only one fight because of a foul—the one refereed by Wyatt.

36 ♦ After being searched at the prizefight, Wyatt was discovered with a concealed weapon and was disarmed before the infamous boxing match began. It's the only time in the history of California boxing that a referee had to be disarmed prior to a fight.

37 ♦ Wyatt was in several barroom fights in Alaska and was arrested more than once. In one, he was charged with assaulting and beating a military policeman.

38 ♦ In 1899, in Saint Michael, Alaska, Wyatt managed a canteen that served only beer (at a dollar a drink) and cigars (at fifty cents each). The bar grossed $200 a day, seven days a week and Wyatt received 10 percent off the top.

39 ♦ In 1911, Wyatt and several others were arrested in Los Angeles, California, for bunco steering (running a phony card game). Wyatt was ultimately absolved of complicity but gave the police a false name, William Stapp. The police department tagged him as a "professional gambler and all-around sharper." The *Los Angeles Times* labeled Earp as a card sharp who "devoted his time to fleecing the unwary in card games" and claimed it was Wyatt who conceived of the plot.

40 ♦ One of those also arrested with Wyatt was Walter Scott, who later talked a rich Easterner into building a castle in the Mohave Desert, which became known as Scottie's Castle.

41 ♦ Wyatt served as a movie consultant on several films, most notably those of William S. Hart and Tom Mix. (This is where the plot from the movie *Sunset*—starring James Garner as Wyatt and Bruce Willis as Tom Mix—came from.)

42 ♦ Wyatt and his third wife Sadie (late in life she would demand to be called Josie) wintered across the river from Parker, Arizona, for numerous years up until the late 1920s. Marion Beaver, an old-timer in Parker, remembers Wyatt walking across the railroad trestle over the Colorado River to come into town for rhubarb pie.

43 ♦ Wyatt periodically traveled from his Happy Days Mine (located near Vidal, California) to Needles, California, where he would join in card games and invariably fleece soldiers on their payday.

44 ♦ Photos of Wyatt's favorite camping spot (near his Happy Days Mine) show that the legendary frontiersman set up camp in a wash. This is the last place anyone who knows about flash floods would camp. Even worse, in the book *I Married Wyatt Earp*,

Mrs. Earp tells of a flash flood almost washing them away (Wyatt's brother ended up in a tree). Wyatt's lack of knowledge about the dangers of the desert boggles the mind.

Even in his 70s, Wyatt was still game to fleece soldiers on payday in Needles, California.

45 ♦ Late in life, Wyatt decided to pursue culture and read Shakespeare. His com-ment: "That feller Hamlet was a talkative man. He wouldn't have lasted long in Kansas."

46 ♦ In Wyatt's feeble attempts at writing his life story (he dictated his memoirs to a secretary named John Flood, Jr.), he overused the word "Crack!," a popular replacement for "Bang!" When describing the classic O.K. gunfight in Tombstone, Earp used "Crack!" 102 times to depict how many shots were fired.

47 ♦ The historical record says "around 30" shots were fired at the gunfight near the O.K. Corral. Earp claimed in his autobiography: "So rapid were the flashes [from the guns] that the heat of the metal extended back into the butts of the forty-fives until the palms of the gunners began to burn."

48 ♦ President Teddy Roosevelt was indirectly responsible for making Wyatt Earp an Old West icon. The president invited various Old West characters to the White House (Geronimo and Pat Garrett, to name two). When Bat Masterson visited, he told Teddy, "The true story of the West will never be known until Wyatt Earp talks." Roosevelt's press secretary, Stuart Lake, overheard these remarks and later went West to find the 80-year-old former lawman. The resulting book, *Wyatt Earp: Frontier Marshal*, posthumously enshrined Earp in the pantheon of Western icons. Thanks to that book (and Walter Noble Burns' book, *Tombstone*), Wyatt now stands shoulder to shoulder with the legendary Buffalo Bill Cody and Wild Bill Hickok.

49 ♦ Wyatt's last words were, "Suppose...suppose...."

50 ♦ Wyatt was cremated, and his ashes are buried in a Jewish cemetery in Colma, California, beside his third wife Sadie.

THE WILD BUNCH

WILD, BUT NOT MUCH OF A BUNCH

WHO was the Wild Bunch? What crimes can be attributed to the gang? And who participated in those crimes? These questions defy simple answers.

EYEWITNESSES ARE UNRELIABLE AT BEST, and they are especially dodgy regarding masked perpetrators. Witnesses to Wild Bunch crimes disagreed on descriptions, even on how many bandits were involved. Those indicted were usually acquitted. So how can we, over a century later, determine the truth? We can only try.

On June 24, 1889, Butch Cassidy, Matt Warner and Tom McCarty (abetted by others, perhaps including Bill Madden and Butch's brother, Dan Parker) robbed the San Miguel Valley Bank in Telluride, Colorado, of around $20,000. Considering that trio as the root of the Wild Bunch, we can fold in later crimes in which they participated.

The Last Supper of Outlaw Photos. ***The "Fort Worth Five" is today's label for this iconic 1900 photograph of a quintet of Wild Bunch members (from left to right) Sundance Kid, Will Carver, Ben Kilpatrick, Harvey Logan and Butch Cassidy. "The Curse of the Fort Worth Five" would be a more accurate title. All five men died violent deaths.***

Tom McCarty and Matt Warner along with Tom's brothers Bill and George, his nephew Fred, his brother-in-law Hank Vaughan and George's wife Nellie staged about 10 holdups in Oregon, Washington and Colorado between 1890–93. The outlaws' tastes were catholic: They hit trains, banks, casinos and stores. The gang dissolved after Fred and Bill died during an 1893 attempt on the Farmers and Merchants Bank in Delta, Colorado.

The Rocky Mountain branch of the Wild Bunch made an inauspicious start on November 29, 1892, near Malta, Montana, when three men—probably the Sundance Kid, Harry Bass and Bill Madden—held up the Great Northern No. 32 and netted less than $100. Bass and Madden were caught and implicated Sundance, who had escaped.

Butch Cassidy's outlaw career resumed in 1896, after he had finished serving a two-year prison term for horse theft. On August 13, he, Elzy Lay and Bub Meeks robbed Idaho's Bank of Montpelier of $7,165. The money went to attorneys defending Matt Warner for murder. On April 21, 1897, Butch, Lay and perhaps Meeks and Joe Walker stole a $9,860 mine payroll in Castle Gate, Utah.

On June 28, 1897, six bandits flubbed a holdup of the Butte County Bank in Belle Fourche, South Dakota. Tom O'Day was caught hiding in a saloon privy. His cohorts included Walt Punteney, George "Flat Nose" Currie, Harvey Logan (making his debut in the Wild Bunch) and Sundance. Butch may have participated, but it is doubtful. The bungling bandits got only $97. O'Day was tried and acquitted; Punteney was arrested, but the charges against him were dropped.

Butch's reputation outpaced his criminal record. In a story headlined "King of the Bandits," a Chicago daily declared in early 1898 that "Butch Cassidy is a bad man." Not just any bad man, but "the worst man" in Utah, Colorado, Idaho and Wyoming, the leader of a gang of 500 outlaws "subdivided into five bands."

On July 14 that year, a trio of bandits, said to have been Sundance, Logan and Currie (though they were never identified), held up the Southern Pacific No. 1 near Humboldt, Nevada, escaping with $450. Two other men were tried for the holdup and acquitted.

Wyoming Territorial Prison where Butch was incarcerated from July 1894 until January 1896 for horse theft. He was by all accounts a model prisoner, and upon release, he became a model bandit.

The Humboldt threesome struck again on April 3, 1899, robbing a saloon in Elko, Nevada, of several hundred dollars. The Wild Bunch holding up saloons? Maybe not. (Unsolved crimes are often attributed to famous outlaws.) Three local cowboys were tried for the robbery and acquitted.

Meanwhile, other outlaws were roaming the Southwest. Three Texas delinquents, Tom "Black Jack" Ketchum, Dave Atkins and Will Carver, held up a Southern Pacific train near Lozier, Texas, on May 14, 1897, taking upwards of $42,000. Reinforced by Tom's brother Sam and possibly

THE WILD BUNCH

CRIME AND PUNISHMENT

Matt Warner
Train & bank robber & murderer
Died of natural causes, 1938

Will Carver
Train & bank robber
Shot dead, 1901

Tom O'Day
Bank robber
Wagon accident, 1930

Bill McCarty
Train & bank robber
Shot dead, 1893

William Ellsworth "Elzy" Lay
Train & bank robber & murderer
Natural causes, 1938

Harvey Logan
Train & bank robber & murderer
Suicide, 1904

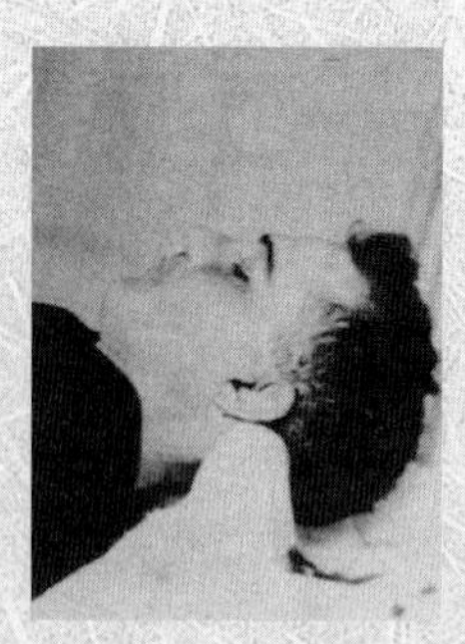

Lonnie Logan
Train robber
Shot dead, 1900

Tom "Black Jack" Ketchum
Train robber & murderer
Hanged, 1901

Dave Atkins
Train robber
Natural causes, 1964

Union Pacific railcar after the Wild Bunch dynamited it in a 1900 holdup near Tipton, Wyoming.

Bruce "Red" Weaver, they robbed the Gulf, Colorado & Santa Fe No. 1 on September 3, of several thousand dollars. Weaver was later tried for the crime and acquitted.

Success bred carelessness. On December 9, five bandits, probably the Ketchum brothers, Carver, Atkins and Edward H. Cullen, attempted to rob the Southern Pacific No. 20 near Stein's Pass, New Mexico, but met a fusillade from armed guards. Cullen was killed; the other four, though wounded, escaped. Unchastened, four men—probably the Ketchum brothers and perhaps Carver and Ben Kilpatrick—robbed the Texas Pacific No. 3 at Mustang Creek, Texas, on July 1, 1898, grabbing between $1,000 and $50,000 in cash. (Victims were not forthcoming about how much was stolen. Sometimes employees pocketed overlooked money and included it in the amount said to have been taken by the bandits. At other times, initial accounts lowballed the sums, and the truth came out decades later.)

Elzy Lay joined the gang just in time for its train-robbing blitz to come to a bloody halt. On July 11, 1899, Sam Ketchum, Lay and Carver overpowered the crew of the Colorado & Southern No. 1 and galloped off with some $30,000. (Weaver, thought to have been standing guard nearby, separated from the others.) After the holdup, the three principals were surprised by a posse. When the dust settled, one posse member was dead and two were wounded, one mortally; Ketchum was mortally wounded; Lay was wounded and later captured; and Carver escaped. (Some say the third bandit was Harvey Logan, not Carver.)

Tom Ketchum, meanwhile, picked an inauspicious moment to launch a solo career. On August 16, he attempted holding up the Colorado & Southern No. 1 near Folsom, New Mexico, but was shot, captured, tried, convicted and hanged.

These calamities should have been a lesson to Carver and Kilpatrick, but they merely moved north and joined the Wild Bunch proper.

The first crime that consolidated what was left of the various gangs was the June 2, 1899, robbery of the Union Pacific Overland Flyer No. 1 near Wilcox, Wyoming. This holdup, which yielded between $3,400 and $50,000, made the Hole-in-the-Wall Gang nationally famous. "They were lawless men who have lived long in the crags and become like eagles," averred the *New York Herald*. Yet, we can't place Butch or Sundance at the scene with any precision. Witnesses reported six masked men; most historians count George Currie, Harvey Logan, his brother Lonnie Logan and their cousin Bob Lee among them.

The Sundance Kid and his paramour Ethel Place had this photo taken in 1901 at the De Young Studio in New York City. On February 20 that year, Sundance, Ethel and Butch Cassidy sailed for Argentina.

The lawless eagles swept down again on August 29, 1900, robbing the Union Pacific Overland Flyer No. 3 near Tipton, Wyoming, of between $55.40 (the initial account) and $55,000 (a later report). The five bandits included Butch and probably Sundance and Harvey Logan. Also suspected were Ben Kilpatrick, Tom Welch and Billy Rose. Tipton was the first crime in which Butch and Sundance are generally agreed to have teamed up. They were just six months from fleeing the country.

Three weeks later, on September 19, three or four bandits struck the First National Bank in Winnemucca, Nevada, collecting between $32 and $40,000. Sundance, Carver and Logan are thought to have participated, but some suspected local miscreants, and others called it an inside job. The bank's head cashier, George Nixon, at various times agreed and disagreed that Butch was present. A few years later, a newspaper recounted a conversation in which Sundance supposedly disclosed that he, Butch and Carver were responsible. Stories that the bandits had camped near Winnemucca as early as September 9, however, have prompted researchers to question whether Butch and Sundance could have been at both Tipton and Winnemucca, 600 miles apart.

Butch and Sundance left for Argentina in February 1901. Today popularly considered the leaders of the Wild Bunch, they had teamed up on only two or three robberies. As crime sprees go, it was not much of a run. Their colleagues sputtered on, but within a couple of years, most were dead or in jail.

On July 3, 1901, what was left of the gang on North American soil attacked the Great Northern Coast Flyer No. 3 near Wagner, Montana, fleeing with about $40,000. There were four to six bandits, including Harvey Logan, Ben Kilpatrick and O.C. Hanks. Kilpatrick and Logan went to prison for passing bank notes from the holdup, and Hanks died the next year in a confrontation with authorities in Texas.

Logan, who had escaped from jail in 1903, rounded up two friends, probably from Ketchum territory, for what would be his farewell appearance, the botched holdup of the Denver & Rio Grande near Parachute, Colorado, on June 7, 1904. Wounded and cornered, Logan committed suicide. The list of possible accomplices is long, but George Kilpatrick (Ben's brother) and Dan Sheffield are high on it. George is thought to have been mortally wounded, although his body was never found.

WILD BUNCH BY THE NUMBERS

20+
Wild Bunch murders.

100+
Years gang members spent behind bars.

15
Members who died with their boots on.

3
Wild Bunch members who committed suicide.

6
Wild Bunch members who did time in prison, got out, then got themselves killed.

2 OR 3
Number of holdups in which Butch and Sundance teamed up in the U.S.

2
Number of robberies in which Butch and Sundance teamed up in South America.

1
Number of people Butch Cassidy killed.

1
(Maybe)
Number of people the Sundance Kid killed.

The northern hemisphere's Wild Bunch was kaput, except for one footnote. Ben Kilpatrick, released from prison in 1911, joined former cellmate Ole Beck to rob the Galveston, Harrisburg & San Antonio No. 9 near Sanderson, Texas, on March 13, 1912. Quick-witted Wells Fargo messenger David Trousdale fatally bludgeoned Kilpatrick with an ice mallet, borrowed his rifle and dropped Beck.

So, what was the Wild Bunch? Between the late 1880s and early 1900s, there were several gangs, comprising several dozen outlaws, who are part of the Wild Bunch story. The McCarty-Warner and Ketchum Gangs had more coherence than the Rocky Mountain Wild Bunch, perhaps because they were family based. All the bandits put together committed or attempted more than two dozen holdups. They probably didn't do some they've been blamed for, and they probably pulled others they've never been accused of.

Of the approximately 20 outlaws who can be counted in the Rocky Mountain Wild Bunch during its heyday, the 1896–1901 Montpelier to Wagner era, few participated in crimes together more than a couple of times, and the gang's holdups in that period numbered a scant five to seven. Butch and Sundance—surprisingly, given their later iconic status as a joined-at-the-holster outlaw duo—teamed up in the United States no more than three times. If they hadn't gone to South America and died together, the 1969 movie *Butch Cassidy and the Sundance Kid* would never have been made, nor this story written.

Last known photograph of Butch and Sundance in the Bolivian Andes, circa 1907. Butch is astride his mule and Sundance is tending to his.

THE COMING OF THE SACRED DOG

HOW INDIANS OF THE AMERICAN WEST GOT THE HORSE

"THE *God of the Christians is dead.*

He was made of rotten wood."

These words, allegedly uttered in his native language by

Tewa holy man Popé, marked the beginning of the Indian

renaissance in North America.

FOR SOME TIME, POPÉ HAD BEEN telling his fellow Pueblos that the source of their woes was the Spanish: If the Indians drove these bearded interlopers from their homeland, rejected Christianity and returned to their ancestral ways, their life would again be good.

In 1680, the holy man finally united the independent Pueblo communities to his cause. Rebelling against Spanish cruelty, the natives revolted, driving their conquerors out—at least temporarily—and launching a massive change in Indian culture.

BOWING TO THE "YOKE OF CHRIST"

Decades before Popé's declaration, Spanish conquistadors, led by Juan de Oñate, had introduced Christianity to the Pueblo Indians of the Rio Grande watershed. In 1598, Oñate, the newly appointed governor and captain-general of New Mexico, led a force of eight Franciscan friars and about 130 soldiers (plus their families and servants—around 400 people, altogether) into the valley of the Rio Grande, home to an estimated 50,000 Indians, who lived in 60 villages or pueblos, as their communities were called.

In 1610, Santa Fe—the city of Holy Faith—became the capital of the New Mexico colony, igniting a land rush of retired Spanish soldiers, who received large land grants for their former service. The soldier/settlers built *haciendas* on their new *rancheros* and pressed the

For nomadic tribes, horses enhanced a preexisting way of life, replacing dogs for carrying heavy loads. Horses also allowed Indians to kill buffalo individually, as dramatically portrayed in John Inness'* The Buffalo Hunt, *instead of killing them en masse at buffalo jumps.

Pueblo Indians who had been living there into servitude. Of course, other soldiers were always on hand to see that the Pueblos complied with the wishes of their Spanish masters.

. . . they also raided the Apaches for slaves to export to Mexico's silver mines.

Catholic priests also "taxed" the Pueblos for their labor, requiring them to build churches and tend clerical farms. The friars' demand for native labor often put the priests at odds with the Spanish settlers, who felt the Indians' time would be better served working for them, writes historian Geoffrey C. Ward in *The West*. The Franciscans further angered the Pueblos by ordering them to put aside their tribal religion and instead bow to the "yoke of Christ." Publicly, the Indians paid lip service to Christianity, while within their kivas—underground rooms used for native ceremonies—they worshipped their traditional gods.

In addition to planting corn, melons and other crops for their Spanish masters, the Pueblos also tended the Spaniards' enormous herds of cattle, sheep and horses (called "sacred dogs" by some of the Plains Indians because the horses looked like magical dogs that could carry heavy loads).

The Spanish livestock caught the attention of the Apaches, who had begun moving into the region from the East in the late sixteenth century. Although the Apaches traded with the Pueblos, they also raided them for plunder, particularly horses and mules. Initially, the Apaches ate most of the animals they captured, but they soon began bartering their surplus to the Kiowas and other neighboring tribes. Before long, Spanish horses and their offspring were being swapped from tribe to tribe through a vast Indian trading network that extended north to the Missouri River and into Canada.

From the West, Navajos, like the Apaches, also raided the New Mexico *rancheros* for horses. From the Navajos, horses passed through the Utes to the Shoshonis and on to the Nez Perce and other tribes of the Northwest plateau country.

Rather than chase the horse thieves, the Spanish replaced their losses by importing more stock from their *rancheros* in central Mexico. A typical small Mexican ranch of the period had over 150,000 cattle and 20,000 horses, reports Ethno-historian Alfred W. Crosby in *The Columbian Exchange*.

Although stolen horses filtered through the Indian trading network, their numbers were too few to alter native life on the Northern Great Plains. For the most part, tribes such as the Blackfeet, Crows and Assiniboines continued to be pedestrian nomads who used dogs as their beasts of burden. But all of that was about to change.

THE GREAT PUEBLO REVOLT

During the 70 years after the founding of Santa Fe, various Spanish governors, settlers and their priests systematically looted the Pueblo Indians of New Mexico. Not only did the Spanish steal Pueblo land and labor, but they also raided the Apaches for slaves to export to Mexico's silver mines. In retaliation, the Apaches, who also sold captives to the slavers, stepped up their attacks on the Spanish-controlled Pueblos.

MEDICINE MAN'S LEDGER DRAWINGS

In 1875, the federal government imprisoned leading warriors of four tribes in hopes of quelling Plains Indian unrest. While a prisoner at Fort Marion in St. Augustine, Florida, 33-year-old Cheyenne warrior artist Making Medicine created ledger drawings showing how Plains Indians depended on horses for their survival.

(From left) Near camp, Indians on horseback hunt buffalo, while the next scene shows a rider thrown from his horse during the hunt. In order to kill the buffalo, riders must catch up to the herd, but sometimes while riding at full gallop, horses stumbled in prairie dog holes, as indicated in this drawing where the hoof print is drawn inside a circle (center right edge). Because the Cheyenne were dependent on the buffalo, they had to follow the wandering herds. In this next drawing, you can see horses dragging travois, which were crossed tipi poles used for carrying the Indians' belongings. But the buffalo was not the only animal Cheyennes hunted from horseback, as shown in Making Medicine's drawing of Indians riding down antelope.

During the seventeenth century, smallpox, measles, diphtheria and other European diseases also beset the Pueblos. In 1638, one-third of all Pueblos—perhaps as many as 20,000 people—died, most probably from smallpox. Two years later, disease claimed another 10,000. And then in the 1660s, the rains stopped, as the Pueblos' homeland entered a period of prolonged drought.

Frustrated, small pockets of Pueblos began lashing out at their Spanish masters, who retaliated in 1675 by charging 47 Indian leaders with witchcraft. All were beaten and three were hanged when they refused to submit to Spanish authority. The Spanish would have sold the surviving prisoners into slavery, including Popé, the Tewa holy man, Ward writes, had not a large group of armed Pueblos interceded on their behalf. Rather than risk his outnumbered soldiers (at the time, there were fewer than 3,000 Spanish of all ages in New Mexico) in a lopsided fight, New Mexico Gov. Juan Francisco de Treviño released Popé and the other captives.

On August 10, 1680, the Pueblo Indians revolted en masse, killing 21 of New Mexico's 33 Franciscan priests and 375 (some reports say as many as 500) Spanish settlers. Terrified, the remaining Spanish barricaded themselves in the Palace of Governors in Santa Fe, while Pueblo warriors laid siege to the building and razed the rest of the town.

For 11 days, the Spanish huddled together inside their adobe fortress before finally fighting their way through the Pueblos and fleeing southeast to the mission at El Paso del Norte. It would be 12 years before the Spanish would regain control, but during the dozen years they were gone, Popé initiated the Plains Indian renaissance.

"SACRED DOGS" INCREASE MOBILITY

Having orchestrated the Spanish defeat, Popé appropriated the governors' palace in Santa Fe for his own. Vowing that the good life would return to their homeland if the Pueblos abandoned all things Spanish, he ordered his followers to embrace their traditional religious ceremonies and renounce Catholicism. He also demanded that the Pueblos destroy the Spanish-introduced fruit orchards and other European crops, and that they cast aside their metal hoes—which helped produce more bountiful harvests—in favor of those made from antler and bone. And most significantly for the Indians of the Great Plains, Popé insisted that the Pueblos empty the Spanish *rancheros* of their vast horse herds.

Almost overnight, what had once been a trickle of stolen horses in the Indian trading network became a floodtide of horseflesh. Native Americans acquired most of their horses "as a result of the Pueblo Indian uprising of 1680," writes Herman J. Viola in *After Columbus: The Smithsonian Chronicle of the North American Indians.*

As more and more tribes obtained horses, their mobility increased. The Sioux, who lived in the Minnesota lake country, changed from what Viola describes as a "canoeing people" to some of the "greatest light cavalry history has ever known." Pressured by their Ojibwa neighbors, the Sioux began a multiyear exodus from their traditional homeland to the Western Plains. Buffalo became their staple, as they increasingly hunted from horseback.

Horses now allowed Plains tribes to travel farther afield and much faster than ever before. Horses also altered native hunting patterns. Instead of killing buffalo at buffalo jumps, Indian warriors could kill them from horseback. Because a buffalo cow's meat was more tender to eat than a bull's and a cow's hide was easier for Indian women to tan, mounted Indians began hunting more selectively, especially when buffalo were plentiful. This changing ratio of cows-to-bulls-killed—especially from 1830–60, during the peak years of the buffalo robe trade—eventually altered the sexual composition of the herds.

Because Indians viewed horses as wealth, they naturally sought to acquire more, both through breeding and by stealing from their neighbors. Horse raids now became an important means for warriors not only to build larger herds but also to acquire status within their tribes. Needing grazing land for their growing number of horses, Indians often drove the buffalo from the prime grasslands, which further stressed the buffalo herds.

The use of horses also altered the traditional trading patterns of tribes such as the Nez Perce. Now when they traveled from their plateau homeland in Eastern Washington and West-central Idaho to the Montana prairie in order to hunt buffalo, they could carry more than just enough supplies to satisfy their subsistence needs. Packing their horses with excess salmon oil, salmon pemmican, camas bread, hemp twine and composite bows (laminated with horns from bighorn sheep), they traded with the Blackfeet, Crows and Assiniboines for catlinite pipes, war bonnets and similar truck. (It was common for tribes to put aside their traditional hostility with their neighbors in order to trade.) Just as free trade raises the living standard of nations world-wide, it did so for all trading-oriented tribes in North America.

THE CORONADO MYTH

The belief that Plains Indian horse herds were descendants of animals that escaped or were captured from Spanish explorers Francisco Vasquez de Coronado and Hernando de Soto is a myth, according to historian Frank Gilbert Roe in *The Indian and the Horse.* Only two of Coronado's 558 horses were mares, and they were not lost. Conquistadors were required by Spanish law to ride stallions. Instead, most of the horses came from the Spanish *rancheros* in New Mexico, following the Pueblos' revolt.

SPANISH RULE RETURNS

Although the wide use of horses began a renaissance among the tribes of the Great Plains and Northwestern plateau country, the same was not true for the Pueblos, who had traded off the Spanish stock. They had merely exchanged one despot for another. Popé ordered all churches destroyed and all Christian-sanctioned marriages absolved. Crosses, rosaries and everything else "tainted" with Catholicism were to be smashed or burned, and those Indians who had been baptized were commanded to wash themselves clean.

Decreeing that the Spanish language was never again to be uttered, Popé began wearing elaborate costumes and adorning his head with the horn of a bull. Pueblos who failed to heed the holy man's dictates were imprisoned or executed.

As the Pueblos seethed under their new taskmaster, many noticed that the rain did not return as he had promised. The traditional crops of corn, squash and beans that Popé had ordered them to plant withered under the boiling sun just as the Spanish crops of peaches, melons and grapes had done before the revolution.

Popé died in 1688, whether from natural causes or at the hand of the Pueblos is unknown. Four years later, the new governor, Don Diego José de Vargas Zapata Luján Ponce de León y Contreras, led a retinue of 60 soldiers, 100 loyal Indians and several friars back to Santa Fe, arriving on September 13. The Pueblos at Santa Fe welcomed the Spanish, and by December, when Vargas returned to El Paso for more soldiers, over 2,000 Indians had been baptized.

This formal portrait of Spanish conquistador Don Diego José de Vargas Zapata Luján Ponce de León y Contreras celebrates his role as a peacekeeper (he persuaded the Pueblos to surrender to Spanish rule in 1692). Yet, a year later, Vargas ordered scores of the Pueblo leaders shot during their rebellion.

Following Vargas' arrival in Santa Fe late the next year, a number of Pueblos again sought to drive the Spanish out, but this time, they failed. By December 1696, all rebellion had been quashed.

Although the Pueblos were again under Spanish rule, their rebellion had ushered in a time of prosperity for the Indians of the Great Plains and Northwestern plateau country. As more and more tribes obtained the horses (or their offspring) that Popé had ordered out of New Mexico, intertribal trade increased and living standards rose. The first eight decades of the 18th century were the apex of the American Indian renaissance, a time of plenty that would be abruptly ended by the great smallpox epidemic of 1780–81.

"IF THEY'RE HUNGRY, LET THEM EAT GRASS"

THE INSIDE STORY BEHIND AMERICA'S GREATEST MASS HANGING

WHEN *you think of the savagery of the Old West, Minnesota doesn't leap to mind. Montana, yes; South Dakota, yes; Arizona, yes, but not a Midwestern state that sits on the eastern edge of the West.*

YET, MINNESOTA PLAYED A PIVOTAL ROLE in the bloody conflict between whites and Indians that spanned nearly three decades: it was here that the first great Plains Indian war began; that one of the most notorious Indian uprisings took hundreds of lives; and where America saw its "greatest mass execution."

The state was only four years old—most of its young men were off fighting the Civil War—when it was thrust into a second "war within a war in its own backyard," one that catapulted Minnesota into what became known as the "Great Sioux Uprising of 1862."

This event launched a series of Indian wars on the Northern Plains that didn't end until the Battle of Wounded Knee in 1890. But Minnesota is where it started.

And hunger began it.

NEAR STARVATION

The crops had failed in 1861, and that winter had been one of near starvation for the Sioux who had sold 24 million acres of rich agricultural land and now lived on reservations, existing on the annuity payments for their property, which totaled some $3 million. But the 1862 payments that normally came in late June and early July didn't arrive. By mid-August, Indians began showing up at agency headquarters, demanding food from the warehouses, which they would pay for once their checks came.

Some agency officials gave them food; others were stingy. Storekeeper Andrew J. Myrick callously remarked, "If they're hungry, let them eat grass." He would die for those words.

But it was a trivial egg-stealing incident that mushroomed into war: six weeks of bloody, brutal fighting that took the lives of at least 450 white settlers and soldiers—and maybe as many as 800—and a couple of dozen Indian warriors.

Andrew J. Myrick

CHICKEN EGGS

As Chief Big Eagle told it, hunting had been unproductive for four weary and hungry Sioux warriors one hot August morning when they chanced upon a nest of chicken eggs near a farmhouse. One warrior took the eggs despite his companions' warning that stealing from the whites would cause trouble. Dashing the eggs to the ground in anger, he shouted, "You are afraid of the white man, you are afraid to take eggs from him even though you are starving."

According to Big Eagle, a companion angrily replied, "I am not afraid of the white man and to show I am not, I will go to his house and shoot him. Are you brave enough to go with me?" The others agreed to accompany him to the nearby homestead of Robinson Jones in Acton Township. Cunningly, they challenged Jones and his neighbors, Howard Baker and Veronius Webster, to test their marksmanship. A target was placed on a tree and the Indians and whites emptied their rifles at the mark. The Indians immediately reloaded, but the white men neglected to take that precaution. Suddenly, the Sioux turned on the settlers and brutally shot down Webster, Baker, Jones and his wife and Clara Wilson, their adopted daughter.

The four culprits, later identified by Big Eagle as Brown Wing, Killing Ghost, Breaking Up and Runs Against Something While Crawling, stole several horses and fled to their Rice Creek village on the Minnesota River. It was obvious to everyone that this was a bad situation—white women had been killed, which surely meant retaliation and possibly no more annuity checks.

Colonel Henry Sibley

THE GREAT SIOUX UPRISING OF 1862

Some chiefs immediately wanted to go to war; others urged caution, but all agreed only Little Crow had the ability and prestige to lead a successful attack.

Riders summoned Chiefs Mankato, Wabasha, Traveling Hail and Big Eagle to the home of Little Crow. As related by Big Eagle, Little Crow told the council, "Braves, you are like little children: you know not what you do. You are full of the white man's devil water, you are like dogs in the hot moon that snap at their own shadows. We are like little herds of buffalo; the great herds are no more. The whites are as many as the locusts. Kill one or ten whites and ten times ten will come to kill you. Count your fingers all day long and the whites with guns will come faster than you can count." Little Crow's admonitions—which history would prove to be prophetic—went unheeded, so he reluctantly agreed to lead the uprising.

The carnage began immediately. Small bands of Indians swooped down on unsuspecting homesteaders. The men were quickly gunned down and axed by the warriors while the women and children were assaulted and either killed or taken captive. After plundering the homes and barns, the Indians burned the farms and fields.

Encouraged by their early successes and the whites' feeble response, the Indians turned their attentions to the settlements. Anticipating an easy victory, several hundred armed and painted Indians surrounded Lower Agency. The unarmed whites were quickly overwhelmed.

Andrew Myrick was among the first to die. He was found near his home, his mouth stuffed with grass.

The Sioux swept through the Minnesota Valley in an orgy of killing, raping, looting and burning. The whites who survived told of the bone-chilling war whoops that accompanied unmerciful attacks on loved ones. Panicked homesteaders fled to the larger settlements for safety, often relying on the walls of brick buildings to survive. One hotel, the two-story Dacotah House, "was so crowded, the women had to remove their hoop skirts."

One hero, a Christian Indian named John Other Day, led 62 whites across the river to safety. In retaliation, the Indians burned his farm and destroyed his crops. After the uprising, a grateful government awarded him $2,500 for his bravery.

The last significant battle occurred on September 23 when Col. Henry Sibley, who commanded a force of 1,619 men, faced off against 1,000 Indians. Sibley's command camped at Battle Lake near present-day Echo. That night, the Sioux stealthily approached. At dawn, the raiders attacked in a fan-shaped formation, yet Capt. Mark Hendrick's howitzers "mowed down the Indians like grass."

It was a decisive victory for Col. Sibley. In a letter to his wife, he stated the Indians "received a severe blow and will not be able to make another stand." His assumption was correct. There would be no more organized warfare by the Sioux in Minnesota. Now, the troops could concentrate on release of the captives and capture of the troublemakers.

Sibley was concerned Little Crow would kill all the hostages and indeed, the Sioux chief wanted to do just that. Fortunately, by this time, Little Crow's influence had waned and the Indians refused to carry out his wishes. Chiefs Wabasha and Taopi were desperately trying to end the hostilities, and Little Paul, a highly respected Sioux orator, spoke strongly in favor of ending the warfare and releasing the prisoners. As a result, Wabasha sent Joseph Campbell, a mixed-blood (people of mixed Indian and white ancestry), to let Sibley know the captives were safe and the soldiers could come for them.

MILITARY TRIAL—"A TRAVESTY OF JUSTICE"

The captives were held at a camp near the mouth of the Chippewa River near Montevideo. It quickly became known as Camp Release. Sibley, with an escort of troops, entered the Indian Camp, "with drums beating and colors flying." An eyewitness wrote, "The poor creatures, half starved and nearly naked, wept with joy at their release." The rescued numbered 269—mostly women and children—the men having been killed.

Sibley sent most of the rescued to Fort Ridgely; orphaned children were sent to settlements near their homes and most were adopted by relatives. Some women remained at Camp Release to testify at the trials of the Indians.

Nearly 2,000 Sioux were taken into custody and trials began almost immediately. A five-man military commission, headed by Col. William Crooks, prepared to try the accused.

Joseph Godfrey, a mixed-blood, greatly aided the prosecution. Godfrey was the first person tried and sentenced to hang, but his sentence was reduced to 10 years imprisonment when he agreed to testify. Intelligent and articulate, he helped convict many Indians.

Executive Mansion,

Washington, December 6th, 1862.

Brigadier General H. H. Sibley
St. Paul
Minnesota.

Ordered that of the Indians and Half-breeds sentenced to be hanged by the Military Commission, composed of Colonel Crooks, Lt. Colonel Marshall, Captain Grant, Captain Bailey, and Lieutenant Olin, and lately sitting in Minnesota, you cause to be executed on Friday the nineteenth day of December, instant, the following names, to wit

"Te-he-hdo-ne-cha." No. 2. by the record.
"Tazoo" alias "Plan-doo-ta." No. 4. by the record.
"Wy-a-tah-to-wah" No. 5 by the record.
"Hin-han-shoon-ko-yag." No. 6 by the record
"Muz-za-bom-a-du." No. 10. by the record.
"Wah-pey-du-ta." No. 11. by the record
"Wa-he-hua." No. 12 by the record
"Sna-ma-ni." No. 14. by the record.
"Ta-te-mi-na." No. 15. by the record.
"Rda-in-yan-kna." No. 19. by the record
"Do-wan-sa." No. 22. by the record.
"Ha-pan" No. 24. by the record.

"Hda-hin-hday." No. 373. by the record.
"O-ya-tay-a-koo." No. 377. by the record.
"May-hoo-way-wa." No. 382. by the record.
"Wa-kin-yan-na." No. 383 by the record

The other condemned prisoners you will hold subject to further orders, taking care that they neither escape, nor are subjected to any unlawful violence.

Abraham Lincoln, President of the United States.

President Abraham Lincoln (above, circa 1861) wrote out the 39 Sioux to be hanged on Executive Mansion stationery. (One Indian was later granted a reprieve.) The first and last page of the three-page executive order are shown above.

(Godfrey was released after three years and farmed peacefully near Niobrara, Nebraska, until his death in 1909.)

Urged to hurry, the commission settled as many as 40 cases each day, some lasting just five minutes. "Reading the records today buttresses the impression that the trials were a travesty of justice," writes Kenneth Carley in his 1976 account of the uprising for the Minnesota Historical Society. "It is true that those in charge had to resist public pressure to do away with all the Indians, guilty and innocent alike, and it must also be pointed out that the trials were conducted by a military commission and not by a court of law. Nevertheless, many of the proceedings were too hasty and quite a number of prisoners were condemned on flimsy evidence."

On November 5, the commission finished its work. Of 392 Indians tried, 307 were sentenced to hang and 16 were given prison terms. Col. Sibley approved all but one death sentence—the exception being the brother of John Other Day.

Most of the Indians were naive and couldn't understand why they were being punished for honorable warfare. Many offered ridiculous extenuating circumstances. Some admitted firing only one or two shots, but argued they never hit anyone because they were such poor shots and their guns were inaccurate. Others claimed to be eating corn during the battles, while some had bellyaches and weren't able to join the fighting. One admitted stealing a horse, "but it was a very small one."

PRESIDENT LINCOLN NAMES THE CONDEMNED

Sibley wanted to execute the condemned at once but was unsure of his authority. Therefore, on November 7, he forwarded a list of the condemned and complete records of their convictions to President Abraham Lincoln. The president received many appeals from the press, Minnesota Gov. Alexander Ramsey and others urging immediate execution. Episcopalian Bishop Henry Whipple was one of the few who urged clemency: "This affair must not be settled with passion, but by calm thought."

Lincoln heeded the advice of those seeking mercy and on December 6, 1862, commuted the death sentences of all but 39 warriors who had been convicted of wanton murder and rape. The president's decision—he hand-wrote every name on Executive Mansion stationery—was unpopular with most Minnesotans. (One man on the list would later get a reprieve, leaving 38 to die.)

The condemned were held at Camp Lincoln, but when enraged citizens threatened "frontier justice," the Indians were moved to a more secure jail in Mankato to await execution on December 26.

On Christmas Day, families of the 38 were allowed a last visit. Most of the Indians were resigned to their fate. Rdainyanka, son-in-law of Chief Wabasha and a leader in the uprising, eloquently wrote his father-in-law, "I am set apart for execution and will die in a few days. My wife and children are dear to me. Let them not grieve for me. Let them remember that the brave should be prepared to meet death and I will do as becomes a Dakota."

At dawn on December 26, the 38 began chanting their death songs. Their chains were removed and their arms were bound with ropes. At 10 A.M., they were taken from the prison to the huge wooden scaffold. Martial law had been declared, and 1,400 soldiers surrounded the condemned. Thousands of civilians thronged the area to watch the proceedings. To a slow, measured drumbeat, the Sioux climbed the stairs of the scaffold. At the end of the third drum roll, William Duley, an uprising survivor, stepped forward and cut the rope to release the traps. As the 38 dropped to their deaths, there was a prolonged cheer from the soldiers and citizens. This would become known as "America's greatest mass execution."

SIOUX WAR AFTERMATH

Little Crow, leader of the uprising, was conspicuously absent from the trials and punishment. When the fighting ended, he had fled to Canada. In June 1863, accompanied by 16 warriors, Little Crow returned to Minnesota to steal horses. It would be his last foray. Several whites were killed at this time, and Little Crow's band was assumed responsible. On July 3, the chief and his son Wowinapa were ambushed near Hutchinson by Nathan and Chauncey Lamson. Little Crow was killed and taken to Hutchinson where he was scalped, mutilated and buried in a pile of offal. In 1971, he received a more dignified burial when his remains were interred at Flandrau in a quiet ceremony. Little Crow's grandson, 88-year-old Jesse Wakeman, said, "We decided Ta-O-Ya-Te-Dutah [Little Crow] should be buried among his own with only his own on hand."

Shown here in 1858, Little Crow, the Sioux leader in the uprising, was picking berries near Hutchinson, Minnesota, when he was killed by Nathan and Chauncey Lamson in 1863.

The executions weren't the end of the Sioux Wars. Minnesotans retaliated against all Indians, whether they'd been involved in the uprising or not. "The Sioux Indians of Minnesota must be exterminated or driven forever beyond the borders of the state," Gov. Ramsey declared. He demanded, and Congress agreed, that the Indians' annuity money should be spent to compensate white victims of the uprising (even though some of the claims were so extravagant, they were outrageous).

The Minnesota government even persecuted a peaceful Winnebago tribe that had taken no part in the Sioux War. That the Winnebagos "lived on choice farm lands coveted by the whites raises a presumption that the settlers may well have been prompted by economic motives, coupled with fear and prejudice in wanting to get rid of the unfortunate Winnebago," Carley writes.

And of course, this was just the beginning of blood that would flow for decades. As Carley reports, "The Minnesota Uprising of 1862 was still fresh in the nation's memory when it became aware of such Indian leaders as Red Cloud, Sitting Bull and Crazy Horse. Bloody battles at Fort Phil Kearny, the Little Bighorn, and, in 1890, Wounded Knee, brought to an end at last the generation of Indian warfare that had begun at Acton in August, 1862."

THE WARRIOR WHO KILLED CUSTER?

THE CONTROVERSY STILL RAGES

IN *the last seconds of his life on June 25, 1876, Lt. Col. George Armstrong Custer tried to bite off the nose of the man who was killing him.*

CUSTER PUT UP A BRAVE FIGHT, right to the end, which made the kill all the more heroic for the 26-year-old Sioux (Dakota) warrior who was the nephew of Sitting Bull.

This story of those last moments wasn't publicly told until 81 years after the rash young commander and over 200 of his cavalrymen were wiped out in the infamous Battle of the Little Bighorn.

The man who told it was the only one who could have possibly known: Joseph White Bull, who detailed how he had been the one who killed "Long Hair." Some believe he was right; others say that although he fought at Little Bighorn, there's no evidence any of the soldiers he killed included Custer.

But here's how he told it: "I charged in. A tall, well-built soldier with yellow hair and mustache saw me coming and tried to bluff me, aiming his rifle at me without shooting. I dodged it. We grabbed each other and wrestled there in the dust and smoke. It was like fighting in fog. This soldier was very strong and brave. He tried to wrench my rifle from me. I lashed him across the face with my quirt [riding whip], striking the coup [the warrior scored honor points by touching his enemy]. He let go, then grabbed my gun with both hands until I struck him again.

"But the tall soldier fought hard. He was desperate. He hit me with his fist on the jaw and shoulders, then grabbed my long braids with both hands, pulled my face close and tried to bite my nose off. I yelled for help: 'hey, hey, come over and help me!' I thought that soldier would kill me."

Is Lt. Col. Custer Long Hair? (circa March 1876)

Those astonishing words first appeared in a 1957 article in *American Heritage Magazine*. The story was written by historian Stanley Vestal, who had published a biography on Sitting Bull in 1932 and then a biography on White Bull two years later. Vestal, whose real name was Walter Stanley Campbell, said he omitted the explosive information about Custer from White Bull's biography to protect the aging Indian, who by then was a chief. But by

BUILDING THE AMERICAN WEST

February 8, 1861
After 11 states secede from the Union and establish the Confederate States of America, former U.S. Secretary of War Jefferson Davis is elected the first president.

Cattle Kate: 1861–89.

April 12, 1861
Confederates fire on Fort Sumter, starting the Civil War.

July 2, 1861
Ellen Liddy Watson (later known as Cattle Kate) is born in Canada.

July 15, 1861
Wild Bill Hickok is charged for the murder of David McCanles. Claiming self-defense, Hickok is acquitted.

October 24, 1861
The nation's first transcontinental telegraph line is completed. The Pony Express ends two days later.

1862
The remaining Sioux (Dakota) Indians are driven from Minnesota, following their defeat at the Battle of Woods Lake. Wild Bill Hickok becomes a Union spy.

January 10, 1862
Samuel Colt dies.

January 1, 1863
President Abraham Lincoln issues the Emancipation Proclamation.

January 29, 1863
California Union volunteers commanded by Col. Patrick Connor attack Shoshonis near Southeastern Idaho's Bear River, killing 368 (more than double the number of Indians killed at Sand Creek or Wounded Knee).

October 3, 1863
President Lincoln proclaims the last Thursday in November to be a national holiday of Thanksgiving.

November 19, 1863
President Lincoln gives his "Gettysburg Address."

J.L.G. Ferris' painting of the first Thanksgiving.

January 6, 1864
Army troops led by former mountain man Kit Carson route the Navajos from their Canyon de Chelly stronghold.

1957, White Bull had been dead a decade and Vestal himself would die later that year. In one of the final articles the esteemed historian wrote, Vestal said he was coming clean with information he'd kept secret all those years.

White Bull told the story himself in a "ledger book" he produced in the early 1930s for North Dakota Congressman Usher Burdick. White Bull's ledger book was part of the exhibition "Plains Indian Drawings, 1865–1935" that toured American and Canadian museums in the late 1990s, organized by the American Federation of Arts.

White Bull being interviewed by George Bird Grinnell (center) and William Rowland.

In his ledger book—named for the humble business ledgers that white traders gave to Indians to record their drawings and stories—White Bull includes four pictographs on Custer's demise as well as text written in the Teton Dakota language.

That text was first translated by Vestal, who kept references vague about the soldier White Bull had killed. Later, in Vestal's magazine story, the historian included a more complete description of the fight, based on interviews with White Bull.

"Bear Lice and Crow Boy heard me call and came running," White Bull's story continues. "These friends tried to hit the soldier. But we were whirling around, back and forth, so that most of their blows hit me. They knocked me dizzy. I yelled as loud as I could to scare my enemy, but he would not let go. Finally I broke free.

"He drew his pistol. I wrenched it out of his hand and struck him with it three or four

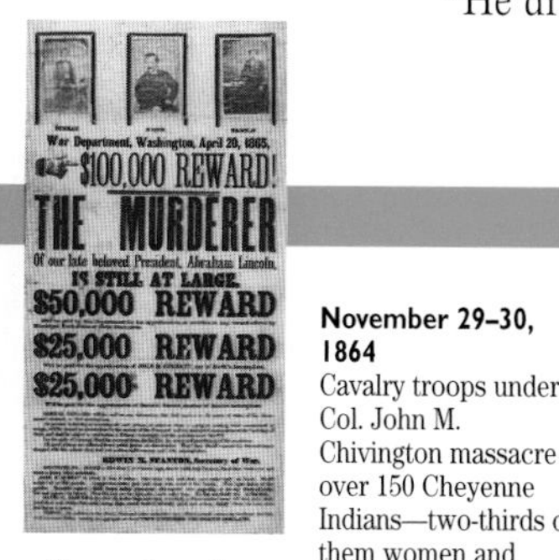

Reward poster for Lincoln's assassin.

1861-1880

November 29–30, 1864
Cavalry troops under Col. John M. Chivington massacre over 150 Cheyenne Indians—two-thirds of them women and children—at Sand Creek in Southeastern Colorado.

March 1865
Pierre Chouteau, Jr. & Company sells out to the Northwest Fur Company, essentially ending the fur-trading era on the Upper Missouri River.

Judge Roy Bean with the four children he had with his wife Virginia.

April 14, 1865
John Wilkes Booth shoots President Lincoln at Ford's Theatre in Washington, D.C. Lincoln dies the next morning.

May 5, 1865
In North Bend, Ohio, bandits derail a train, rifle the express car and rob the male passengers in the first recorded civilian train holdup in the United States.

October 28, 1866
"Judge" Roy Bean marries Virginia Chavez in San Antonio, Texas.

December 21, 1866
Captain William J. Fetterman and his entire command are killed by Sioux warriors under Crazy Horse and Red Cloud.

February 1867
Harper's New Monthly Magazine carries a story inflating the exploits of Wild Bill Hickok.

Sec. of State Seward.

March 30, 1867
Secretary of State William H. Seward formalizes the purchase of Alaska from Russia for $7.2 million. A skeptical public terms the sale "Seward's Folly."

1868
Commissioner of Indian Affairs puts the cost of the Indian Wars at $1 million for every Indian killed.

times on the head, knocked him over, shot him in the head, and fired at his heart. I took his pistol and cartridge belt. Hawk-Stays-Up struck second [coup] on his body.

"Ho hechetu! That was a fight, a hard fight. But it was a glorious battle. I enjoyed it. I was picking up head-feathers right and left that day."

White Bull said at that moment, he didn't know who he had just killed, but a relative who knew Custer by sight identified the body.

In his ledger book, White Bull refers to Custer as "Long Hair" (Custer's nickname, even though he'd cut his hair before the battle) and writes: "Long Hair charged the camp and there was a lot of confusion and gunfire. Many Dakotas were killed as a result of this first charge and this made them mad. We counterattacked. We fought with them and I was in the first assault wave. My friend, maybe you can tell me how many of them we killed. Maybe you can tell me how many Dakotas were killed. . . . Long Hair came charging in but I pulled him off his horse. He was lying at the east end. At first they ran, but I chased them. That's when I did it, while the excitement was going on. It was wonderful. I was twenty-six years old at the time. My horse was a fast one. It was a great fight."

Returning to the fight, White Bull adds, "He stood pointing his carbine at me and I was afraid but I charged him and ran him down. He fired at me but missed. It was lucky for me. This was a hard fight, the hardest I ever fought, but finally I overpowered him. I have had this in my memory for a long time. Now I have shown it to you, friend. Many of the Dakotas and the white men saw me do this and know me, my friend."

In a third pictorial that he identifies as referring to Long Hair, White Bull shows himself "counting coup" on the soldier, writing, "This deed was seen by others who will vouch for me and verify that I am telling the truth, my friend."

And in the fourth picture, he says, "I grabbed him and killed him. I counted first coup. He hit me with his fists and hurt me and then he grabbed my braids. I grabbed his carbine and killed him with it. I was scared but I finally succeeded. The soldier was Long Hair."

In 1960, late historian James H. Howard headed the translation of White Bull's ledger book under a grant from the University of North Dakota. It resulted in Howard's book, *Lakota Warrior*. Howard would later write that he came away believing White Bull was "our most likely candidate" as the warrior who killed Custer.

Chicago, after the fire.

BUILDING THE AMERICAN WEST

May 10, 1869
Crews from the Central Pacific and Union Pacific Railroad Companies complete the transcontinental railway at Promontory, Utah.

August 30, 1869
John Wesley Powell completes his epic voyage through the Grand Canyon.

April 30, 1871
Angered by continual Apache raids, 148 Papago Indians, Mexicans and Tucson, Arizona, whites attack 500 peaceful Apaches at Camp Grant (Arizona), killing and mutilating upwards of 150 men, women and children.

October 8–11, 1871
Fire rages in Chicago, eventually destroying over 3.5 square miles, killing upwards of 250 people and leaving about 100,000 homeless. Fire may have been started by the O'Leary's cow.

1872
Yellowstone becomes the nation's first national park. John Henry "Doc" Holliday graduates from a Baltimore, Maryland, dental school. Buffalo Bill Cody gives his first performance on stage in *The Scouts of the Prairie*, a Ned Buntline drama.

May 1, 1873
U.S. Post Office issues the first postcard, which costs a penny.

September 1873
Financial panic sweeps the New York Stock Exchange. During the subsequent five-year economic downturn, over 5,000 businesses fail.

July 20, 1874
Army command authorizes Gen. Philip Sheridan to pursue hostile Indians unconditionally, officially beginning the Red River War.

Hickok's grave.

1876
H.J. Heinz Company of Pittsburgh, Pennsylvania, introduces its new tomato "Ketchup." The telephone is patented.

June 25, 1876
Lt. Col. George A. Custer and his entire command are killed by the Sioux at the Battle of the Little Bighorn.

On the 25th anniversary of the battle, Cheyenne Chief Two Moon visited Custer's Hill. During the battle, he was one of a number of Indians who carried a repeating rifle.

Others aren't convinced, believing it is just the word of one Indian and his biographer. And even though White Bull specifically identifies "Long Hair" in four drawings, some insist he was actually talking about four different soldiers and didn't really differentiate between Custer and his men.

Custer expert Paul Hutton says, "It's such a great story, but I don't believe it. White Bull is very reliable, but he never said he killed Custer. It's Stanley Vestal who claimed White Bull killed Custer, and he [Vestal] never let a good story go."

What is not in dispute is that Joseph White Bull was an acclaimed warrior.

He was born in 1849 in the Black Hills, the son of Miniconjou Chief Makes Room and Good Feather Woman. She was a sister of the famous Hunkpapa Dakota medicine man, Sitting Bull. There was a younger brother named One Bull.

In a 1995 article in *American Indian Art Magazine*, authors Ray Miles and John R. Lovett wrote about the ledger book exhibit that was about to start its tour: "As historical documents, these drawings depict a critical period in Lakota history. White Bull's first drawings show him attacking both settlers and soldiers along the Bozeman Trail. The traffic along this trail disrupted the buffalo on prime hunting grounds, which in turn threatened the very basis of Lakota life."

1861 - 1880

August 2, 1876
Jack McCall murders Wild Bill Hickok in Deadwood's #10 Saloon.

September 7, 1876
The James Gang botches the holdup of the First National Bank in Northfield, Minnesota.

May 5, 1877
Sitting Bull and his band of Hunkpapa Dakotas cross the border into Canada.

Ed Schieffelin: Tombstone founder.

August 1, 1877
Ed Schieffelin records his Arizona silver claim, naming it "Tombstone."

February 18, 1878
In Lincoln County, New Mexico, English-born rancher John Tunstall is murdered, precipitating the Lincoln County War.

October 15, 1878
Thomas A. Edison founds the Edison Electric Light Company, a forerunner of today's General Electric Company.

March 4, 1879
New Mexico Gov. Lew Wallace places Billy the Kid (listed as Kid Antrim) on a list of wanted men.

November 1, 1880
Virgil Earp becomes the Tombstone assistant town marshal.

November 2, 1880
Pat Garrett is elected sheriff of Lincoln County, New Mexico.

December 1880
Billy the Kid escapes capture by Pat Garrett and his posse before finally being arrested December 23 at Stinking Springs, east of Fort Sumner, New Mexico.

Billy the Kid escapes capture.

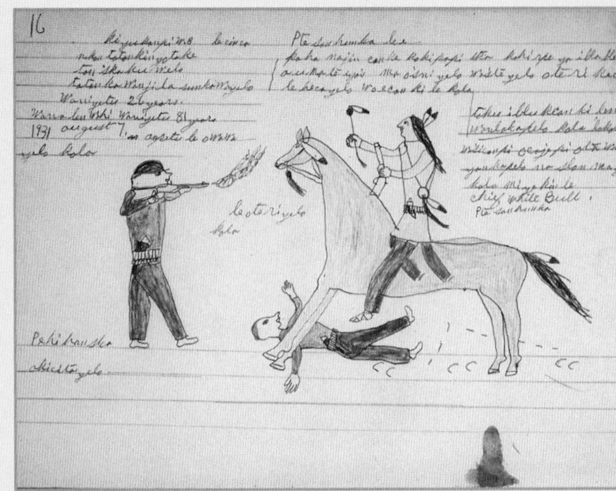

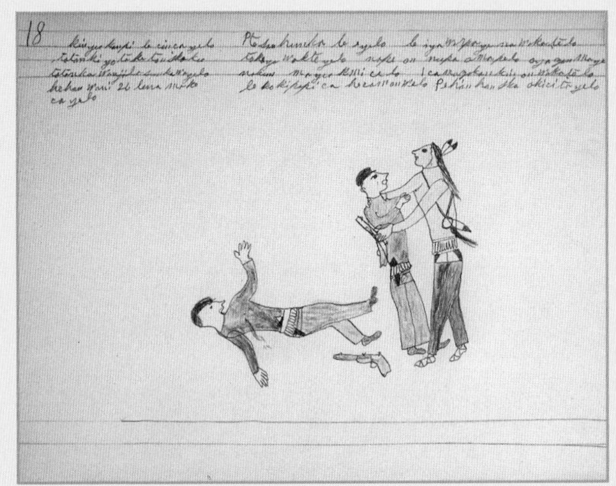

WHITE BULL KILLS CUSTER

Four drawings from White Bull's "ledger book." In I, White Bull pursues a soldier who is attempting to wrestle the carbine from White Bull's grasp. Beneath them lies a soldier, which the text represents as being Custer "lying at the east end"; in II, White Bull charges at a trooper (supposedly Custer) firing at him with a carbine. White Bull is now carrying a stone-headed war club, and his horse is decorated with a scalp hanging from its bridle. The text between the two combatants translates to, "This is Long Hair, the soldier" (note in the drawing, he has short hair); in III, White Bull counts coup on the fallen Custer, who is wounded in the groin; in IV, White Bull and Custer are wrestling to the death. The fallen soldier, with his carbine laying beside him, is said to represent Custer at the end of their struggle.

White Bull

They note that White Bull participated in the four best-known military engagements of the entire period: the Fetterman Fight (December 1866), the Wagon Box Fight (August 1867) and in June 1876, the Battle of the Rosebud and the Battle of the Little Bighorn.

"All of these encounters were part of the larger struggle to keep white intruders off Lakota land," they wrote. "In addition, several of White Bull's drawings depict events of intertribal warfare and raiding against the Crow, Flathead and Assiniboin."

Joseph White Bull became famous long before anyone considered he could be the warrior who killed Custer. In fact, the issue hadn't even been raised when the nation was first attracted to him and his history, during the 50th anniversary of the Battle of the Little Bighorn in 1926.

Vestal had yet to show up at his front door, wanting hours of interviews. No biography had yet been written. North Dakota's congressman hadn't come forward, offering a $50 check for White Bull to produce his ledger book—a check that was never cashed. Until that ceremony, White Bull was just another of the Indians who had been relegated to the reservation after the Dakota wars.

So you have to wonder how he felt that day. Did his secret about Custer at that moment make him walk taller, stride more forcefully?

Perhaps it did, because Chief Joseph White Bull was the one chosen as the "Representative of the Red Race" who led Indian warriors onto the battlefield for the Golden Anniversary ceremony.

JUDGMENT AT JACKSBORO

THE STATE OF TEXAS VS. SATANTA AND BIG TREE

THRONGS *of people descended upon Jacksboro, Texas, on a hot summer day in 1871 to witness a murder trial. Murders were commonplace in reconstruction Texas, but this would be no ordinary event. Cause No. 224 (actually two trials held July 5–6) would be the trial of the century.*

FACING THE GALLOWS WERE KIOWAS SATANTA AND BIG TREE, the first Indians to be tried under white civilian law. Of course, there was no way two Kiowas could receive a fair trial in Indian-ravaged Northwest Texas. On the other hand, it was equally obvious that Satanta and Big Tree were guilty.

Satanta was in his early to mid-50s and Big Tree was about 19 or 20 when they joined prophet and medicine man Maman-ti, Satank and several other Indians as they left their reservation near Fort Sill, Indian Territory. On the Salt Creek Prairie between Belknap and Jacksboro, the warriors waited. Bowing to Maman-ti's vision, the Indians let a military ambulance and mounted riders pass unharmed on May 17. The following afternoon, with a storm brewing, the raiders attacked a train of 10 wagons and 12 teamsters hauling corn. The men were employed by Capt. Henry Warren, who had a government contract delivering supplies to frontier forts.

For the Kiowas, the raid was a moderate success. They suffered a handful of casualties but made off with 41 mules, assorted plunder and six scalps (seven teamsters had been killed, but one was bald).

The ambulance Maman-ti let safely pass on May 17, however, had carried a distinguished passenger: Gen. William T. Sherman, who was touring the Indian frontier and had been on his way to Fort Richardson at Jacksboro. Two teamsters—including wounded Thomas Brazeal—stumbled 20 miles through the rain to report the attack. When Sherman heard Brazeal's story, he immediately ordered Col. Ranald S. Mackenzie of the Fourth Cavalry to pursue the attackers.

Sherman went on to Fort Sill, where with help from Lawrie Tatum, an Indian agent and conscience-troubled Quaker, and Col. Benjamin Grierson's 10th Cavalry, Sherman arrested Satanta, Big Tree and Satank after Satanta admitted taking part in the raid. Maman-ti managed to escape Sherman's net.

Both Sherman and Tatum believed punishing the Indians with the threat of hanging would decrease raids into Texas. "These three Indians should never go forth again," Sherman wrote. "If the Indian Department objects to their being surrendered to a Texas jury, we had better try them by a Military Tribunal, for if from any reason in the world they go back to their tribes free, no life will be safe from Kansas to the Rio Grande."

Col. Ranald S. Mackenzie, who transported the prisoners to Fort Richardson prior to their trial in Jacksboro.

Mackenzie arrived on June 4 and departed with the three Kiowa prisoners four days later. In the lead wagon was the leader of the Koiet-senko warrior society—Satank, who was described by an *Army and Navy Journal* correspondent as "a hoary-headed old sinner sixty years of age or thereabout, grown gray in iniquity and deeds of blood."

Fort Richardson, circa 1872, looking south. Capt. Robert G. Carter made the marks on the photo. The adjutant's office was at the far left and the enlisted men's picket quarters are in the foreground across from Lost Creek.

Covering himself with a blanket, Satank began singing his death song. Using a knife he had procured and his teeth, the warrior slipped free of his manacles. Less than a mile from the fort, he wounded a guard with the knife and grabbed a carbine before being shot to death, "preferring," one newspaper stated, "to die like a warrior than to enter the spirit-land by a dog's death at the end of a rope."

On June 15, Mackenzie's cavalrymen and the two remaining prisoners arrived at Jacksboro to cheers from soldiers and civilians, and music from the regimental band. Satanta and Big Tree were confined at the fort.

WHO'S WHO IN THE TRIAL OF THE CENTURY

Much has been written about Satanta and the trial, but often overlooked are the white principals.

THE COURT

Judge Charles Soward was born in Kentucky in 1836 but had moved to Missouri by 1850. He was admitted to the bar in Canton, Missouri, in 1860 and left for Texas in 1867. Three years later, Gov. Edmund J. Davis appointed Soward judge of the "Jumbo" district comprising Parker, Jack, Palo Pinto, Hood and Johnson Counties.

THE PROSECUTORS

Samuel W.T. Lanham served as prosecutor, with **W.M. McConnell** acting as second chair against Big Tree and **Captain C.L. "Charley" Jordan** assisting against Satanta. A veteran of the Third South Carolina Infantry, Lanham had married Sarah Meng in 1866, and they moved to Texas, where they taught school and he studied law. Admitted to the bar in 1869, he began practicing in Red River County, and Gov. Davis appointed him attorney of the "Jumbo" district. The Indian trial began one day after his 25th birthday.

THE DEFENSE ATTORNEYS

Soward assigned **Thomas Ball** and **Joseph A. Woolfolk** as defense attorneys. Ball had attended William and Mary College and was admitted to the Virginia bar in 1858. He practiced law until receiving a lieutenant's commission in the 47th Virginia Infantry in 1861. In 1869, he moved to Texas.

Kentucky native Woolfolk was educated at St. Mary's College, the University of Missouri and the University of Louisville law school. He first arrived in Texas in 1858 as a surveyor and served as Young County clerk until the Civil War broke out. He was elected second lieutenant of a ranger company stationed at Fort Belknap but later received a commission in the Confederate Army. He married Elizabeth Lewis in 1865 and entered his uncle's law office in Louisville, Kentucky, after the war. Two years later, Woolfolk moved his family to Texas, where he farmed and ranched while also practicing law.

Prosecutor Samuel Willis Tucker Lanham.

Not everyone, however, seemed overjoyed at the prospects of such a monumental trial. Eight lawyers—including Samuel W.T. Lanham and Thomas Ball—petitioned Judge Charles Soward of the 13th Judicial District, requesting court not be held at Jacksboro because of the Indian threat.

The petition was denied. Lanham served as prosecutor and Ball was one of the defense attorneys when the court met in the two-story courthouse July 1. On July 4, an indictment was handed down against Satanta and Big Tree for the murder of the seven teamsters. The trial began the following day.

School was dismissed, and people flocked to the courthouse's top floor, where the case would be heard. Satanta and Big Tree arrived from Fort Richardson in a wagon, surrounded by soldiers to prevent anyone from shooting the prisoners. At 8:30 A.M., court was called into session. The defense first entered a motion that the state had no right to try the Kiowas because the Indians were wards of the federal government. Soward rejected the argument but granted the defense's next motion to sever the trials. Big Tree would be tried first.

Ball opened the case with a plea for compassion. The *Dallas Herald* noted his "speeches were at some points most eloquent, and displayed not only a thorough knowledge of the Indian character," but also proved Ball to be a great orator. In the stifling courtroom, he removed his coat as he described the wrongdoings done against Indians since the time of Spanish explorers. He finally asked the jury to let Satanta and Big Tree "fly away as free and unhampered" as an eagle. When this was translated for the Kiowas by Fort Sill interpreter Horace Jones, the Indians grunted and nodded.

Jones, Col. Mackenzie, teamster Brazeal, Sgt. Miles Varily and agency interpreter Mathew Leeper testified for the prosecution. Brazeal told the jury of the attack, Varily identified Kiowa arrows found at the site and Leeper—testifying on behalf of Indian agent Tatum—told how Satanta had boasted of leading the raid. Ball and Joseph A. Woolfolk asked few questions and called no witnesses for the defense. By early afternoon, it was time for closing arguments. If Ball had wowed spectators with his opening oratory, Prosecutor Lanham did the same in his closing. "This is a novel and important trial, and has, perhaps, no precedent in the history of American criminal jurisprudence," he began. The understatement and politeness ended there.

Lanham noted the defendants' "crude and barbarous appearance; the gravity of the charge; the number of the victims; the horrid brutality and inhuman butchery inflicted upon the bodies of the dead." He called Satanta "the arch of fiend of treachery and blood . . . the inciter of his fellows to rapine and murder," while Big Tree was a "tiger-demon who has tasted blood and loves it as his food—who stops at no crime how black soever."

It took the jury half an hour to come back with a guilty verdict. Court was adjourned. Satanta would get his day in court the following day.

Witnesses and testimony were predominantly the same. Yet, the testimony of Jones, reported the *Dallas Herald*, was "more conclusive and direct than that against Big Tree he having, before arrest, harangued his tribe and said: 'Let no Chief claim the credit of killing those seven men in Texas, I am the Big Chief that did that killing.'"

WHAT CAUSED THE WARREN WAGON TRAIN RAID?

In October 1867, Satank (Sitting Bear) and Satanta (White Bear), as representatives of the Medicine Lodge Treaty council, signed a peace agreement restricting the Plains tribes to reservations near Fort Sill, Oklahoma. But the encroachment by Western emigrants reduced the size of the Kiowa reservation and also threatened to destroy the buffalo herds.

"A long time ago this land belonged to our fathers; but when I go up to the [Arkansas] river I see camps of soldiers on its banks. These soldiers cut down my timber, they kill my buffalo; and when I see that my heart feels like bursting," Satanta said at the treaty, as the *New York Times* reported on November 20, 1867.

The army defaulted on many provisions agreed to during the Medicine Lodge Treaty, such as shortchanging Indian rations, not arresting white outlaws who stole Indian property and allowing free, destructive rein to professional buffalo hunters.

In 1868–69, Gen. Philip H. Sheridan's brutal winter campaign forced the Indians to return to their reservations after their homes and horses were destroyed. Rumors of Lt. Col. George A. Custer's troops killing Cheyenne women and children along Oklahoma's Washita River in November 1868 caused Satanta and Lone Wolf to surrender. They were arrested, nearly hanged by the general and rescued by Kicking Bird, who promised that the Kiowas would cease their raids and remain on the reservation.

In 1871, inadequate provisions overruled the Kiowas' fear of army retribution and they again set off to raid settlers. The Warren wagon train attack on May 18, 1871, ignited outrage across the frontier, and Big Tree and Satanta were sent to trial for murder.

Satank died fighting rather than face trial.

The trial of Satanta and Big Tree was the beginning of the end for the Quaker Peace Policy, as the army eventually succeeded in forcing Indians onto reservations. And by the close of the nineteenth century, fewer than 1,000 buffalo roamed the West as they neared extinction. Only two of the four subspecies survived. Today, Plains Indian tribes are raising buffalo herds in an attempt to reawaken the buffalo's importance to their culture.

—Meghan Saar

This time, however, the defendant testified on his own behalf. Satanta, speaking in Comanche interpreted by Jones, pleaded: "I have been abused by my tribe for being too friendly with the white man. I have always been an advocate of peace. I have always wished this to be made a country of white people. . . . This is the first time I have ever faced Texans. They know me not—neither do I know them. If you let me live, I feel my ability to control my people. If I die it will be like a match put to the prairie. No power can stop it."

Satanta promised peace if released, and even said he would personally kill some war-minded Kiowas. The jury, however, found Satanta guilty and sentenced him to death.

The trial of the century was over, but it didn't end there. Bowing to political pressure and fearing Kiowa retaliation if the death sentences were carried out, Soward wrote Gov. Edmund J. Davis on July 10, pleading with him to commute the sentences to life imprisonment. Davis agreed, and on October 16, Satanta and Big Tree were transported to the state penitentiary in Huntsville.

Following the trial, Woolfolk continued practicing law while improving his farm and ranch operation on the Brazos River. Ball went on to become a state senator and assistant attorney general of Texas, but the trial propelled Lanham into the statehouse. He served as Texas governor from 1903–1907 and was the last Confederate veteran to hold that position.

Satanta and Big Tree were paroled in 1873. An infuriated Sherman wrote Davis "that I believe Satanta and Big Tree will have their revenge, if they have not already had it, and that if they are to have scalps that yours is the first that should be taken."

Big Tree, however, settled down. He worked on a supply train after his parole, helped establish the Rainy Mountain Indian Mission and joined the church in 1897, serving as a deacon until his death in 1929.

Satanta, on the other hand, took part in the Red River War of 1874–75 and was shipped back to Huntsville after he surrendered. Other Kiowa leaders were also punished, such as Maman-ti—the real leader behind the Warren wagon train raid. Maman-ti was sent to Fort Marion in St. Augustine, Florida, where he died of consumption in 1875.

Satanta's health quickly faded in prison. Told that he had no chance of parole, he said, "I cannot wither and die like a dog in chains." The following day, October 11, 1878, he slashed himself and was taken to the second-story prison infirmary to stop the bleeding. Left alone, he jumped from the landing to his death.

In many ways, the Kiowa trial became a catalyst for the demise of the Quaker Peace Policy on the reservations and the defeat of the Kiowa nation. As historian Allen Lee Hamilton writes: "Many raids were far more destructive in terms of lives lost and property destroyed than the one that struck Henry Warren's wagons on May 18, 1871, but few if any have had more far-reaching effects."

"TAKE NO PRISONERS"

THE TRAGEDY AT SAND CREEK

THE *late November dawn broke cold and foggy. Below the barren Southeastern Colorado plain, some 600 Arapaho and Cheyenne Indians were camped in a ravine alongside a dry streambed called Big Sandy Creek. Six hours later, a quarter of them—mostly women and children—were dead at the hands of a Colorado volunteer militia. In time, the name Sand Creek would become synonymous with massacre.*

THE 1864 MASSACRE AT SAND CREEK, more than any other Indian conflict at that time, set the stage for the bloody battles yet to come on the American Plains. Among Indians, it stands as a decisive symbol of white-man betrayal, and among the citizens of Colorado, as the worst tragedy in the state's history.

Earlier that year, roving bands of young Cheyenne and Arapaho warriors had raided Eastern Colorado and Western Kansas, causing alarm among the white settlers. Finally, Territorial Gov. John Evans called for a militia to end the Indian problem. The influential press, led by William N. Byers of the *Rocky Mountain News*, called for the "immediate extinction of the Indians."

"The most revolting, shocking cases of assassination, arson, murder and manslaughter that have crimsoned the pages of time have been done by the Indians, in former days and recently—nevertheless we are opposed to anything which looks like a treaty of peace with the Indians. . . . The season is near at hand when they can be chastised and it should be done with no gentle hand," wrote Byers in the *Rocky Mountain News* on September 28, 1864, clearly stating the views of many citizens of the Colorado Territory.

Territorial politics were reaching an explosive level. The powers at large, primarily those in Denver, had lobbied Washington a second time for admission to the Union. The stakes were high, and the obstacles were numerous. Foremost on the minds of the political hopefuls, particularly Gov. Evans and Col. John M. Chivington, were the recent Indian uprisings. Now, with the support of the influential newspaper editor, the course for Coloradoans was clear: eradicate the "Indian problem."

Into this escalating war between the white soldiers and the Indians came the mixed-blood George Bent, who rode with the Cheyenne Dog Soldiers that bloody fall. Torn between the volatile worlds of the white man and the Indian, Bent was the son of fur trader William Bent and his Cheyenne wife, Owl Woman. George

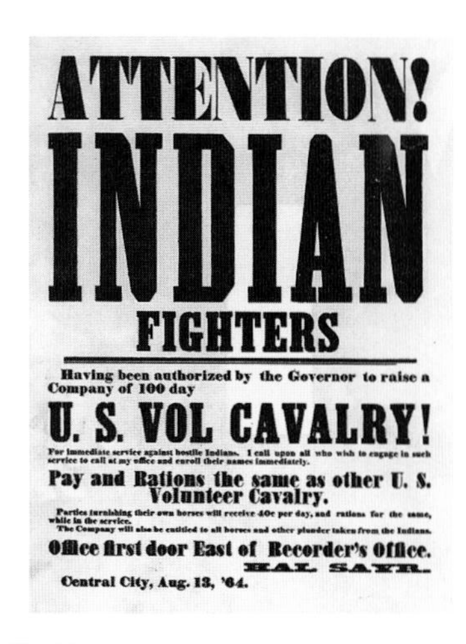

Just one month before the peace meeting, on August 13, 1864, the Central City, Colorado,* Register Call *ran an advertisement for the enlistment of Indian fighters.

BUILDING THE AMERICAN WEST

Much of the Western portion of the transcontinental railroad was built by Chinese labor.

1864
Indians are allowed to testify in federal court. New York streetcar companies end their discrimination against blacks. Thousands of Chinese in Kwantung Province are recruited by the Central Pacific Railroad to work on the Western portion of transcontinental railroad. James Clark Maxwell discovers microwaves. French chemist Louis Pasteur proves his process of pasteurization.

January 10
In Montana, the Vigilante Committee hangs outlaw Sheriff William Henry Plumer on a gallows built by the lawman himself.

Mountain man Kit Carson.

January 13
Stephen Foster, composer of "Camptown Races" and "Oh! Susannah," dies.

January 26
Army troops led by former mountain man Kit Carson route the Navajos, driving them from their Canyon de Chelly stronghold.

February 9
Elizabeth Bacon marries George Armstrong Custer in the Presbyterian Church at Monroe, Michigan.

On that fateful day, the Cheyennes raised American and white flags to signal friendship, which the troops ignored. Instead, the rampaging soldiers crushed Black Kettle's hastily mounted resistance, as portrayed in this 1936 painting by Robert Lindneux.

Newspaper editor William Newton Byers' (left) editorials fed the local hysteria against the Indians.

was born in 1843 at Bent's "Old" Fort, the famous trading post his father had built in Southern Colorado along the Arkansas River. His maternal grandfather was Cheyenne Chief Gray Thunder, the Keeper of the Sacred Arrows. At the age of ten, George and his siblings were sent to St. Louis, Missouri, for their education, where they lived with Albert Boone, grandson of the famous frontiersman. In 1861, George enlisted in the Confederate Army, participating in the

1864

February 17
Confederate submarine CSS *H.L. Hunley* sinks the Union warship *Housatonic* off Charleston. The *Housatonic* is the first warship sunk by a sub.

February 27
The first Northern prisoners arrive at the Confederate prison in Andersonville, Georgia.

March 10
The infamous Jack Slade is hanged by vigilantes at Virginia City, Montana.

Union Ambulance corpsmen load the wounded into their wagons.

March 11
Union Ambulance Corps is established.

March 19
Cowboy artist Charles M. Russell is born.

April 22
The U.S. Congress passes the Coinage Act of 1864, which mandates that the inscription "In God We Trust" must be placed on all coins minted as U.S. currency.

May 11
John A. Huff of the Fifth Michigan fatally wounds Confederate Gen. Jeb Stuart near Yellow Tavern, Virginia.

A young Charles M. Russell, circa 1883.

Territorial Gov. John Evans issued the order, "Go in pursuit of all hostile Indians . . . kill and destroy."

battles at Wilson's Creek and Pea Ridge. Taken as a prisoner after the siege of Corinth, he was eventually released because of pressure from his father's influential friends. Returning to Southern Colorado and his home at Bent's "New" Fort, 22-year-old George soon found himself in the middle of the oncoming war between the two cultures of his life.

William Bent, the first Indian agent in the region, as well as a friend and supporter of his wife's Cheyenne tribe, knew that war was coming. No longer able to reason with Gov. Evans or the soldiers at nearby Fort Lyon, William sent his son to his mother's tribe. George soon learned of the atrocities perpetrated against the Cheyenne by various companies of soldiers, and he began riding with the Dog Soldiers in retaliation.

Colonel John M. Chivington led the Colorado Volunteers to the massacre at Sand Creek.

Cheyenne Chief Black Kettle, widely respected as a fierce adversary of the Pawnee and Kiowa, believed in peace with the white man. In 1861, he had signed a treaty at Fort Wise, promising to remain in the vicinity of the Arkansas River and not to interfere with emigrants along the Smoky Hill Trail, thereby clearing the way for thousands during the Pike's Peak gold rush.

The Cheyennes soon realized that the dry lands near the Arkansas River held little wildlife and that the white settlers had removed much of the area's timber. The young Cheyenne warriors, including George Bent, refused to obey the Treaty of Fort Wise and launched raids among the whites.

BUILDING THE AMERICAN WEST

May 19
Author Nathaniel Hawthorne dies.

June 3
Union and Confederate armies clash at Cold Harbor, east of Richmond, Virginia. Gen. Ulysses S. Grant suffers nearly 7,000 casualties in the first eight minutes; Gen. Robert E. Lee has 1,500 over the entire day.

Nathaniel Hawthorne, author of **The Scarlet Letter.**

June 5
Lotta Crabtree, 17, debuts at Niblo's Saloon in New York City. The Easterners are not impressed with the West Coast sensation, and Lotta leaves the stage in tears. The show closes after six nights.

August 7
Sioux, Cheyenne and Arapaho war parties begin a prolonged attack on stagecoach stations and ranches along the Nebraska portion of the Oregon Trail, shutting off traffic for two months.

August 22
International Red Cross is founded in Geneva, Switzerland.

September 1
Confederate troops evacuate Atlanta, defeated by Union Gen. William Tecumseh Sherman.

September 3
Emil Nobel, the younger brother of Alfred, is killed when Alfred's nitroglycerine factory accidentally explodes.

General Ulysses S. Grant with his wife and son in City Point, Virginia, circa 1864.

When the Nathan Hungate family was found murdered just south of Denver, their scalped and mutilated bodies were brought to Denver and displayed to the public. Mass hysteria gripped the town. (The Cheyenne were later found innocent of the murders.)

Governor Evans issued a general proclamation dispatched to the Indian camps by messengers, ordering all peaceful Indians to assemble at Fort Lyon. Those Indians who did not comply would be killed. The order authorized the citizens of Colorado Territory to "Go in pursuit of all hostile Indians on the plains . . . kill and destroy, as enemies of the country, wherever the Indians may be found."

Evans also wired an urgent plea to Secretary of War Edwin Stanton, requesting authorization for military troops. "Extensive Indian murders, the Indian war begun in earnest," wrote Evans in his wire.

Washington, D.C. gave Evans the authority to enlist citizens for a regiment not to exceed 100 days. In less than a month's time, the Third Regiment of Colorado Volunteers was assembled under the command of Chivington, a local Civil War hero, who had earned praise for his performance at Glorieta Pass.

While Evans stayed busy in Denver recruiting soldiers, Maj. Edward Wynkoop of Fort Lyon met with Black Kettle, who came to the fort in an effort of peace. After much talk, Wynkoop told the chief to bring his people, along with the Arapaho tribes, to the fort for peace negotiations. When Evans heard of the proposed peace talks, he was enraged. Wynkoop later testified that Evans said "it would be supposed at Washington that he had misrepresented matters in regard to the Indian difficulties in Colorado, and he had put the government to a useless expense in raising the regiment; that they had been raised to kill Indians and they must kill Indians." But since Wynkoop had made a promise to the Indians, the governor was forced to meet with them.

"War has begun, and the power to make a treaty has passed," he told the Indian delegation. Chivington ended the peace talks by informing Wynkoop that the Indians "could go to him when they were ready."

Returning to Fort Lyon, Maj. Wynkoop acknowledged the peace tribes of Chiefs Black Kettle, White Antelope, Little Raven and Left Hand, and he told them to camp at Sand Creek, 40 miles north of the fort, as he didn't have enough rations to feed all their people. He also

1864

Mathew Brady captured this scene of Confederate defenses protecting Atlanta.

September 27
Bloody Bill Anderson, leading a band of Confederate guerrillas, including Jesse and Frank James, attacks Centralia, Missouri.

October 31
Nevada is admitted as the 36th U.S. state.

Thanksgiving Day
A Confederate shell sinks Gen. Benjamin Butler's dredge boat on the James River in Virginia.

November 25
An army expedition commanded by Kit Carson fights off several thousand Comanches and Kiowas at Adobe Walls in the Texas Panhandle.

November 29
Cavalry troops commanded by former Methodist minister, Col. John M. Chivington, massacre 150–200 Cheyenne Indians—two-thirds of them women and children—at Sand Creek in Southeastern Colorado.

December 22
Union forces under Gen. Sherman capture Savannah, Georgia.

Two men stand in front of Gen. Butler's sunken dredge boat on Virginia's James River.

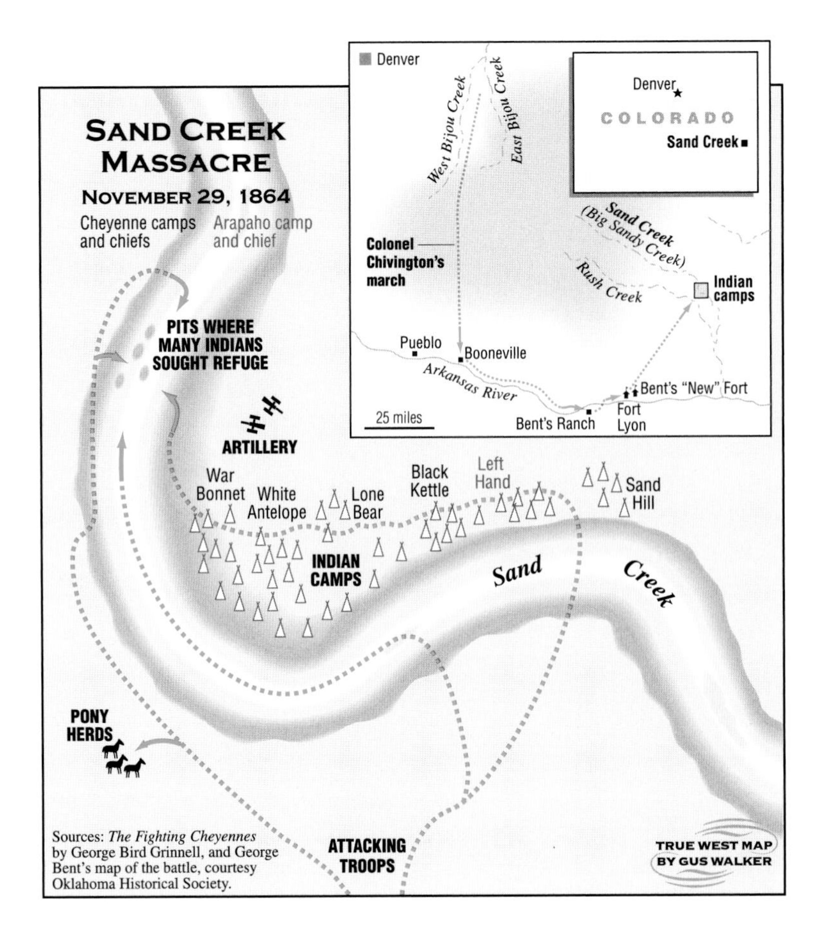

supplied them with firearms to hunt game. Shortly thereafter, Wynkoop was suddenly relieved of his command and replaced by the self-centered, pompous Maj. Scott Anthony.

Evans and Chivington now proceeded with their plan. The new regiment was nearing the end of its 100-day service. Evans and Chivington needed a military victory against the Indians for the citizens of Colorado and their own political agenda. In their minds, both causes were the same; the victory would lead to political triumph.

At camp on Bijou Creek, Chivington rallied his men to the task before them. In a venomous speech, frothed with Indian hatred, Chivington ended by spewing: "take no prisoners. Nits make Lice." Leaving camp, the troops marched doggedly for 200 miles in a severe snowstorm, at times two feet deep.

On the early morning of November 29, 1864, Chivington's troops, together with the Colorado First Regiment—Maj. Anthony's troops from Fort Lyon—charged into Black Kettle's camp. Supporting the armed troops were four 12-pound howitzers.

When the first shots were fired by the troops, fewer than 100 Indians ran up the creek bed to take cover in the rifle pits. The chiefs and the few warriors in camp defended their people as best they could.

As a military operation, the battle was a horrible bungle. Military command was lost early in the day, as soldiers were caught in their own cross fire. The surprised and ill-armed Indians held their own and kept the soldiers at bay for some time. Meanwhile, nearly 500 Indians, including Black Kettle, escaped across the prairie. Those who could not flee died on the spot.

White Antelope was among the first killed. Once the firing began, he left his lodge with arms extended, in the traditional sign of peace, and he was shot down in a single volley of fire.

Eyewitness testimony estimated the number killed to be just under 200, while Chivington boasted 600 "hostiles" were killed, including Chief Black Kettle. Two-thirds of the dead were women and children.

Caught between two worlds, George Bent rode with the Cheyenne Dog Soldiers during the Sand Creek Massacre. Afterwards, he married Magpie, the niece of Chief Black Kettle.

George Bent later recalled, "I looked toward the chief's lodge and saw that Black Kettle had a large American flag tied to a lodge pole. The Indians were all running but they did not seem to know what to do. I got my weapons . . . and joined a group of middle-aged Cheyenne men. We made a stand, but troops came up the west side of the creek and opened hot fire . . . we ran up the creek with the cavalry following . . . I was struck in the hip by a bullet but managed to tumble into a hole. Finally they withdrew, killing all the wounded laying in the creek bed."

As Black Kettle and his wife fled toward the prairie, she was shot. Afterwards, troopers put eight more bullets into her body. A bit later, Black Kettle returned for his wife, and seeing her alive, threw her over his shoulder and ran. By noon, or "when the sun was high in the sky," recounted the Indians, the battle had ended.

Following the massacre, Chivington received a hero's welcome in Denver. It took three years before a Congressional inquest denounced him and his actions.

In October 1867, George Bent served as a witness and official treaty interpreter at the Treaty of Medicine Lodge, where the Cheyenne and Arapaho agreed to allow railroads in the Platte and Smoky Hill Valleys, and to end all attacks against white settlers. In addition, the tribes agreed to exchange their land in the Colorado and Kansas Territories for a reservation in the Indian Territory, which was to be bounded by the 37th parallel and the Arkansas and Cimarron Rivers. Among the Cheyenne leaders to sign the treaty were Black Kettle, Bull Bear, Tall Bull and White Horse.

George Bent later commented: "This is the most important treaty ever signed by the Cheyennes, and it marked the beginning of the end of the Cheyenne as a free and independent warrior and hunter, and eventually changed his old range, from Saskatchewan to Mexico, to the narrow confines of a reservation in Oklahoma."

SWALLOWED BY THE EARTH

SEARCHING FOR PALO DURO CANYON

LAND *has shaped events and people.*

Nowhere is this more true than the

Texas Panhandle's Palo Duro Canyon.

A STRAIGHT HORIZON LINE as far as the eye can see is how best to describe the High Plains of the Texas Panhandle. The tableland was known as the *Llano Estacado* by Spanish explorers and the Staked Plains by Texan frontiersmen battling hostile Comanches. It is a world half made up of pale blue sky and the other half grass—endless grass.

Then, suddenly, there is a massive drop-off into the second largest canyon in the United States. For a million years, the Prairie Dog Town Fork of the Red River ate into the high plateau, slashing open a canyon system up to 1,100 feet deep that stretched for 120 miles and in some spots was 20 miles wide. The cut was deep enough to penetrate the Ogallala Aquifer, an underground lake the size of Lake Erie. The results are cool water running year-round in the shade of the canyon and shadows cast by wind-sculpted pinnacles and turrets.

The natural wonder provided Indian tribes with winter shelter from deadly blizzards and water and grass during the relentless heat of summer. Before the advent of the horse, Apaches set grass fires, driving buffalo herds over the cliffs to the canyon bottom. Hundreds of years later, mounted Comanches and Kiowas did the same.

GRIEF TO CONQUISTADORS

Francisco Coronado was the first European to discover the Palo Duro, during his quest for the golden city of Quivera. The 27-year-old conquistador and his army was led onto the *Llano Estacado* by a Pawnee slave they had rescued in what is now New Mexico. In May 1540, Coronado and his men descended into the canyon.

The Spanish named the canyon Palo Duro, meaning "hard wood" after the abundance of juniper trees in the area. But Palo Duro brought grief to the conquistadors. When the native Apaches presented the Spaniards with gifts of cured buffalo hides, Coronado's men fought viciously over each other's share. Then, a hail storm with "fist size" ice pellets beat down on the small army, denting armor and injuring numerous horses. On May 26, Coronado decided to strike out from Palo Duro with a small, fast band of 30 horsemen. Coronado sent the remainder of his army back to Mexico. He would never come this way again.

Quanah Parker, son of white captive Cynthia Ann Parker, was one of the last Comanche war chiefs to surrender. He led a combined force of Comanches and Kiowas against Col. Ranald Mackenzie's Fourth Cavalry on the floor of the Palo Duro Canyon on September 28, 1874.

Other Spanish explorers nervously crossed the *Llano Estacado*. The arid flatness, without landmarks to be used for a bearing, made them uneasy as did the now mounted Apaches. When the Comanches moved south into the *Llano*, the Spanish joined them in their war against the Apaches, driving them into their current lands in Arizona and New Mexico. The smaller Kiowa tribe followed the Comanches, making the Texas Panhandle their home as well. The two tribes warred against each other until the 1790s when they decided it was best if each tribe came to the aid of the other. From then on every winter, the Palo Duro Canyon became a home for Kiowa and Comanche lodges. By the 1830s, the lodges of the Southern Cheyennes could also be found in the Palo Duro.

For generations, Comanche and Kiowa warriors charged from out of the Palo Duro in the spring, raiding the Apaches, then the Spanish and finally, Texan settlements to the south and wagon trains to the north. Spanish maps of the *Llano* were inaccurate, while American maps simply showed the Staked Plains as a blank space. Pursuing Texan frontiersmen and U.S. cavalrymen often stated it was as though the hostiles rose up from the ground to attack them and then were swallowed up again by the earth.

RED RIVER WAR

There were rumors from Mexican *ciboleros* (buffalo hunters) and captured *comancheros* (renegade traders) of Palo Duro's existence, but nothing concrete. Texan and, during the Civil War, Confederate forces broke off the chase once the Comanches rode onto the *Llano*. Kit Carson went looking for the Palo Duro in 1864 with his Colorado Mountain Battalion but was driven out after the first battle of Adobe Walls, where he encountered waves of Comanche and Kiowa warriors.

It was obvious to the combatants that somewhere on the Staked Plains was a massive meeting place for their enemies. But where? The U.S. Army decided to search for Palo Duro and destroy whatever they found there during the Red River War of the 1870s.

Five army columns were to converge onto the Staked Plains in 1874: Col. Ranald Mackenzie with the Fourth Calvary from Fort Concho to the south, Lt. Col. John Davidson with a column from Fort Sill in the Indian Territory to the east, Maj. William Price with a third column leaving New Mexico from the west, Lt. Col. George Buell with men from Forts

Wild Bill Hickok quits show business.

1874
First "Sholes and Glidden Type Writer" is introduced to the public; it's produced by gunmakers E. Remington & Sons in Ilion, New York. North America's worst grasshopper plague spreads from Texas to the Canadian border.

January 5
Henry McCarty (a.k.a. Billy the Kid) attends a public school in Silver City, New Mexico.

January 31
The James Gang robs the Little Rock Express train near Gadshill, Missouri.

March 13
Wild Bill Hickok quits Buffalo Bill's Wild West Show and heads west, arriving in Cheyenne, Wyoming, on July 22.

April 24
Jesse James weds his first cousin, Zerelda Mimms, in Kearney, Missouri.

June 8
Chiricahua Apache Chief Cochise dies at Camp Bowie, Arizona.

June 27
Aided by .50 caliber, rapid-fire Sharps rifles, 29 buffalo hunters (including William "Bat" Masterson) hold off 700 Kiowa, Cheyenne, Arapaho and Comanche warriors during the second battle of Adobe Walls in the Texas Panhandle.

June 29
During the battle, Billy Dixon supposedly shoots an Indian from 1,538 yards away with an 1874 Sharps .50-90.

Mrs. Jesse James and her two children, a few days after Jesse was killed.

Mackenzie successfully led his outnumbered Fourth Cavalry against the superior numbers of Comanches, Kiowas and Southern Cheyennes in order to capture and kill their pony herd.

Griffin and Richardson to the southeast and Col. Nelson A. Miles with his command out of Fort Dodge to the northeast.

The five army units ran into a hornet's nest as soon as they rode into the Texas Panhandle. Each column, except Mackenzie's, engaged hostiles either in battle or in hit-and-run raids.

Miles was the first to arrive at the mouth of Palo Duro on August 27 with 600 men. Cautiously entering the winding channels of the canyon, his advance unit of 39 scouts was attacked by an estimated 150 Cheyenne Dog Soldiers. Miles quickly formed his men up with mounted troops to the left, infantry to the right and cannon and gatling guns in the center. Ahead of them, the soldiers could see thousands of Cheyennes, Kiowas and Comanches taking positions along the canyon ridges.

"If a man is killed, I will make him a corporal," shouted Capt. Adna Chaffee, who then ordered his men to charge straight up the center of the canyon.

For five hours, the battle raged as Miles' command slowly pushed 12 miles into the southern end of Palo Duro. When Kiowa Chief Woman's Heart was killed, the Kiowas gave ground but rallied. Finally, Miles had to order a retreat. He had overstretched his supply line from Fort Dodge and could not sustain the attack. With only two dead and 15 confirmed dead among the hostiles, Miles believed he was lucky to be able to withdraw back to Kansas in good order. Price, Davidson and Buell also found the going too tough and began their withdrawal from the Panhandle without finding Palo Duro.

Mackenzie and the Fourth, however, were quietly and discretely making their way up

1874

July 8
Canada's newly formed North West Mounted Police begins its "March West" from Fort Dufferin, Manitoba, to present-day Alberta. The force hopes to avoid the Indian Wars being fought south of the border.

July 12
Near Jacksboro, Texas, Kiowas confront Texas Rangers commanded by Maj. John B. Jones, killing two Rangers: David Bailey and William Glass.

***Frederic Remington's* Canadian Mountie.**

July 20
Army command authorizes Gen. Philip Sheridan to pursue hostile Indians unconditionally.

September 10
Kiowas attack an army supply train commanded by Capt. Wyllys Lyman, killing a sergeant and civilian teamster.

September 12
Scouting party sent by Col. Nelson A. Miles to locate the supply train is trapped in a buffalo wallow. One soldier is killed, and all six will receive the Medal of Honor. (Billy Dixon and Amos Chapman's medals are later revoked because they are not part of the regular army.)

October 18
Winchester receives a patent for a reloading tool for its Model 1873 rifle, which greatly enhances the weapon's usefulness and popularity.

Winchester's Model 1873, "the gun that won the West."

November
President Ulysses S. Grant receives King David Kalakaua of Hawaii—the first king to visit the United States.

November 19
The National Women's Christian Temperance Union is formed in Cleveland, Ohio.

from the south. By way of hanging a captured *comanchero*, Mackenzie had learned the exact location of the canyon and a good idea of the thousands of warriors waiting for him. He had only 468 men, but he had a plan that if carried out would mean he would not have to engage the entire might of the enemy. When he closed within several miles of Palo Duro, 300 Comanches attacked on the night of September 26, trying to stampede the army horses. But Mackenzie had placed sleeping parties within the pony herd, and the Comanche attack failed.

As the Comanches retreated, Mackenzie force marched his men for 12 hours. He knew Comanche scouts would be watching as he bedded down his men. He was still miles from the canyon. But he guessed right that the scouts would hurry back to report that his troopers were bedded down for the night. He waited a half hour then quietly ordered his men back on the move. As the first streaks of light appeared in the morning sky of the 28th, Mackenzie and his unit were on the rim of Palo Duro, staring down on a sea of tipis below. Carefully, they made their way down from the rim in single file along a game trail. Suddenly, an Indian sentry spotted them, fired his rifle and began shouting. He was quickly killed, but it was too late. War chiefs led by Quanah Parker hurried their families back into the canyon as warriors formed up to protect their retreat. Mackenzie ordered part of his force forward to engage the enemy, while Troop A made a two-mile dash up the canyon to the Comanche and Kiowa pony herds. Troops H and L began destroying the winter lodges.

Parker sent a large group onto the rim to flank Mackenzie, but Mackenzie saw the movement and sent Troop H back up the rim, holding off the hostiles and securing his line of retreat. He then ordered the Indian herds taken up out of the canyon. Parker and the other war chiefs counterattacked but were deserted by the Cheyennes, who began rescuing their own pony herds and escaping to the south. By 4 P.M., the Battle of Palo Duro Canyon was over. Mackenzie had lost only a handful of men in the bold raid, while Parker and the others lost roughly 50 warriors and their Cheyenne allies.

Over a half century after he first laid claim to the Palo Duro and started up the JA Ranch, Charles Goodnight (above) was buried near the north rim of the massive canyon in 1929.

More importantly, with winter coming, the Comanches and Kiowas lost their horses and their belongings. The next day, Mackenzie had 1,000 of the captured 1,400 horses shot. For close to a half century, cattlemen called the site of the horse slaughter Mackenzie's Boneyard.

RANCHING ON THE TEXAS PANHANDLE

Mackenzie had broken the back of Indian resistance on the Southern Plains. Without horses for hunting, the Comanches, along with their allies, had no choice but to live on Oklahoma reservations. The Texas Panhandle was now safe for white settlement.

Enter the legendary Charles Goodnight, who was born March 5, 1836, three days after Texas declared its independence. Raised along the Texas frontier, he was a Texas Ranger before joining up with Oliver Loving to blaze the famed Goodnight-Loving Trail shortly after the Civil War.

Goodnight settled down onto a ranch outside Pueblo, Colorado, with a new wife, Mary Dyer, when the Depression of 1873 gripped the nation, plunging beef prices and ruining him. He tried to hold off his creditors by borrowing $30,000 from a Denver brokerage firm owned by Englishman John George Adair. Adair had come to America in 1866, opening his first brokerage firm in New York City. But after a buffalo hunt in Kansas in 1874, he fell in love with the West and set up shop in Denver.

Goodnight failed to save his Colorado ranch. He could not repay Adair, but on hearing of the Battle of Palo Duro, he made a business offer to the Englishman. He would set claim to a ranch within the Texas Panhandle, furnish the foundation herd and operate the ranch if Adair would finance the enterprise and pay Goodnight an annual salary of $2,500. The ranch would be called the JA Ranch after Adair. After five years, Adair would get his money back, two-thirds of the ranch, plus a 10 percent profit.

To his shock, Adair agreed, and with cowhands accepting Goodnight's word they would eventually be paid, he headed a herd onto the Staked Plains looking for a site to begin anew.

He had heard of the Palo Duro during the winter of 1875, when Mexican mustangers working along the Canadian River had told one of his cowhands, Frank Mitchell, about the canyon. Ever probing, Goodnight found it in May 1876. He quickly built a dugout to live in and outposts along all the canyon entrances to look out for rustlers. It was his intention to lay claim to all of the Palo Duro. By now, the Texas Panhandle had two settlements: Fort Elliott along the present-day Oklahoma line, to keep an eye out for escaping Comanches, and Tascosa, an open sewer of horse thieves and outlaws.

Operating to his north was the outlaw Dutch Henry, with 300 men taking horses and cattle from Kansas, Colorado and New Mexico ranches, along with money from a few banks. To his south, a smaller outlaw gang of 20–30 men operated near Caprock.

Goodnight decided to ride into Dutch Henry's camp alone to strike an agreement. Goodnight told Henry that all his men were good shots, but if his gang kept to the north half of the Panhandle, he would keep his cowboys to the south end and there should not be any problems. The outlaw roared with laughter. He said he admired how the "damn old man spoke plainly his intentions while sitting alone surrounded by his men." But Henry agreed and lived up to his word for two years before Bat Masterson rode into the Texas Panhandle and took Dutch Henry back to Dodge City to stand trial.

The horse thieves to the south of Palo Duro gave Goodnight some trouble during the first year of operation until he hanged ten of their number and persuaded the gang to move elsewhere.

After the first winter, Mary Dyer Goodnight came to live in the Palo Duro. The only other woman was 80 miles to the north, Mrs. T.S. Bugbee, another rancher's wife. A two-room log cabin was ordered built for Mary's convenience, and the dugout was abandoned.

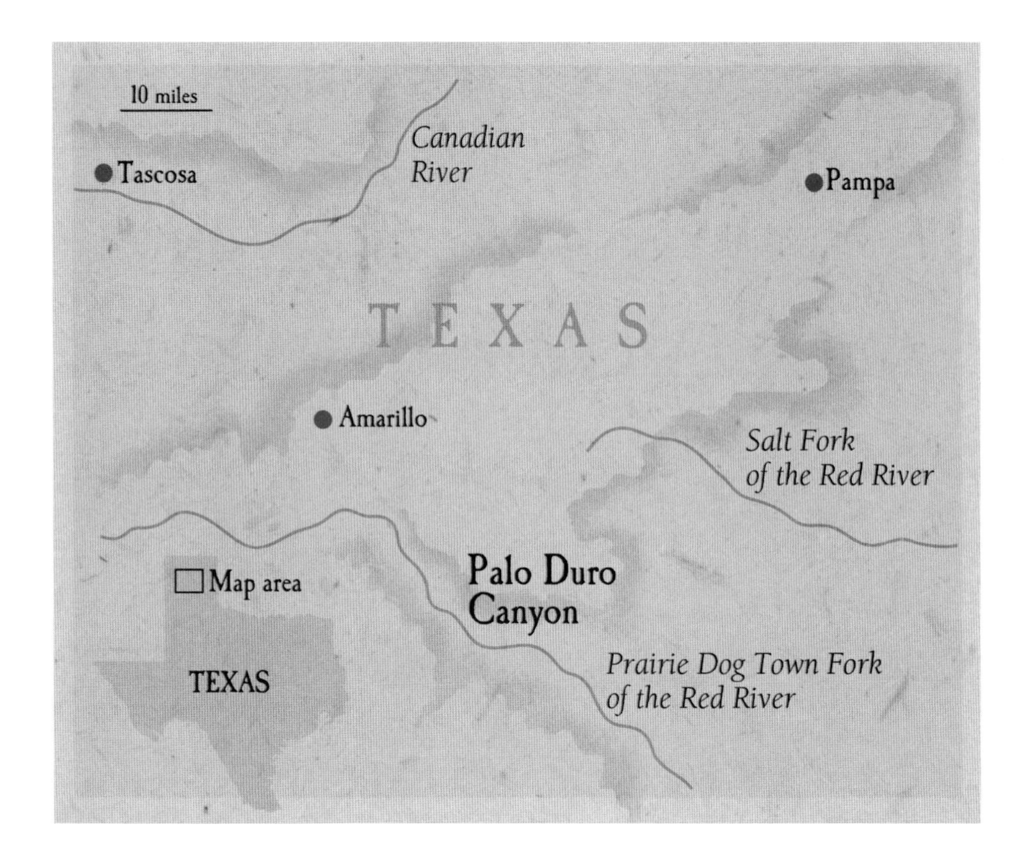

SCOURING THE PLAINS FOR BISON

In the fall of 1878, Quanah Parker and the Comanches returned to the Palo Duro. They had come to hunt the buffalo herds after government rations failed to arrive at their Oklahoma reservation. But in the four years since Mackenzie's raid, hunters had emptied the Staked Plains of bison. Goodnight allowed Parker as much beef as he wanted, but as more Comanche and Kiowa bands began setting up lodges on the canyon floor, the situation grew tense. When an army unit from Fort Elliott arrived on the ranch, Comanche and Kiowa warriors began donning war paint.

Goodnight decided to make some sort of peace agreement. At first, Parker would not listen, questioning if Goodnight was a Tejanos or Texan, the Comanches' sworn enemy. Goodnight told a half-truth, saying he was from Colorado. He managed to get the Indians to leave before winter, and the army returned to Fort Elliott.

Goodnight remained on good terms with Parker. When the Comanche war chief decided to operate his own ranch, it was stocked with JA cattle, courtesy of Goodnight.

A GENERAL NAMED DOROTHY

FIFTY THINGS YOU NEED TO KNOW ABOUT PANCHO VILLA

EVEN *if you don't know exactly who he was, or precisely what he did, you know the name Pancho Villa. He was the most famous Mexican of the Old West.*

BUT WAS HE A HERO OF THE PEOPLE or a ruthless outlaw?

Actually, he was both. And a ladies' man to boot. Here are essentials everyone should know about a general named Dorothy.

1 ♦ Pancho Villa's real name was Doroteo Arango. In Spanish, *Doroteo* is a masculine form of Dorothy. Doroteo adopted the name Francisco Villa after his grandfather, Jesus Villa. (Pancho's father Agustin Arango was the illegitimate son of Villa.) Men whose first name is Francisco are also nicknamed Pancho.

2 ♦ He was born in 1878, at the Rancho de la Coyotada (one of the largest haciendas in Durango; owned by the Lopez Negrete family). He and his family lived the impoverished life of peons.

3 ♦ In his memoirs, Pancho said that at the age of 16 he shot Don Augustin Lopez Negrete, the master of the hacienda, who had reportedly raped Pancho's sister. As the story goes, after wounding his sister's attacker, Pancho fled to the hills and turned rustler and bandit, taking a heavy toll on the herds of the great *ranchos*.

At 22, Pancho was a desperado, earning his nickname as the "Mexican Robin Hood."

BUILDING THE AMERICAN WEST

1901
U.S. sugar sells for 4¢ per pound, eggs for 14¢ per dozen and butter 25¢ per pound. Boardinghouses offer turkey dinner for 20¢ and breakfast and supper for 15¢.

January 22, 1901
Queen Victoria dies after reigning nearly 64 years.

February 20, 1901
Butch Cassidy, the Sundance Kid and Ethel (a.k.a. Etta) Place sail from New York for Argentina.

July 10, 1901
Cole and James Younger are paroled after 25 years in the Stillwater prison.

1905 painting of McKinley's assassination by T. Dart Walker.

September 6, 1901
Anarchist Leon Czolgosz shoots President McKinley at the Pan-American Exposition in Buffalo, New York. The President dies eight days later.

October 24, 1901
Anna Edson Taylor of Bay City, Michigan, successfully goes over Niagara Falls in a barrel. (She was reportedly 63 years old at the time.)

1902
French fashion designer Charles R. Debevoise invents the brassiere. Barnum's Animals (Barnum's Animal Crackers after 1948) are first produced.

Anna Taylor with her barrel.

4 ♦ U.S. Intelligence Agent John Biddle reported that the county sheriff had eloped with Pancho's sister and that Pancho made him dig his own grave before shooting the sheriff and rolling him into it. The report is dated June 12, 1914—20 years after the fact. Whether you believe Pancho's memoirs or Biddle's report is up to you.

5 ♦ Pancho was caught twice by the authorities for shooting Negrete, but he escaped jail both times. To throw off his pursuers, he adopted the name Francisco Villa.

6 ♦ Some writers have declared that Villa was illiterate. Although he had little education, he could read and write well enough to function as a military leader.

7 ♦ While pursuing the life of a desperado, Pancho reportedly stole from only the rich (the poor, of course, had nothing worth stealing).

8 ♦ In 1910, Pancho, now a renowned bandit chieftain, joined the Mexican Revolution. His humble origins made him beloved by poverty-stricken villagers, among whom he recruited his army.

9 ♦ Known as *soldaderas* (women soldiers), the wives of Villa's fighters traveled with the troops, cooked for them and cared for the wounded.

10 ♦ Villa grandly called his soldiers *Los Dorados*—the Golden Ones.

11 ♦ In 1912, Gen. Victoriano Huerta jailed Villa in Mexico City. Villa escaped on Christmas Day and eventually made his way to El Paso, Texas, then a safe haven for Mexican revolutionaries seeking asylum.

12 ♦ One of Pancho's favorite spots in El Paso was the Elite Confectionery. A famous photograph (page 136) shows Villa and his compadres eating ice cream at the Elite.

1901 - 1920

October 24, 1902
On trial in Cheyenne, Wyoming, Tom Horn is convicted of killing 14-year-old Willie Nickell.

November 18, 1902
The Washington *Evening Star* runs a cartoon about President "Teddy" Roosevelt refusing to kill a female bear during a hunt, prompting a couple in Brooklyn, New York, to begin making a brown stuffed animal, dubbed a Teddy Bear.

1903
Edwin S. Porter's film *The Great Train Robbery* is released.

Calamity Jane dies.

May 23–July 26, 1903
The Winton Touring Car, the first automobile driven from San Francisco to the East Coast, reaches New York City.

August 1, 1903
Calamity Jane dies in Terry, South Dakota.

November 20, 1903
Tom Horn is hanged.

December 17, 1903
Orville Wright makes the first successful flight in a mechanically propelled airplane in Kill Devil Hills near Kitty Hawk, North Carolina.

Orville Wright slips the surly bonds of Earth.

Generals Villa and Pascual Orozco (seated across from Villa, with his hat on his knee) at the Elite Confectionery, El Paso, Texas, 1913. Villa and Orozco commanded Francisco Madero's forces and without authority, captured Ciudad Juarez, Chihuahua, on May 10, 1911, which convinced Dictator Porfirio Diaz to resign on May 25. Not wanting to demoralize their forces by retreating southward, Villa and Orozco had ignored Madero's peace treaty with the dictator, which didn't demand Diaz's resignation.

November 21, 1904
In Paris, France, motor-powered omnibuses replace horse-drawn carriages.

March 1, 1905
Milner Dam begins operation, providing water to Southern Idaho farmers. Nearby Twin Falls becomes an overnight boomtown. The project is a showcase for the Carey Act.

April 18–20, 1906
San Francisco earthquake and resulting fire kill about 3,000 people and destroy $500 million in property.

Fork-wielding Mary Mallon. Target: health official Dr. Soper.

1907
New York cook Mary Mallon becomes known as Typhoid Mary after the source of a typhoid epidemic is traced to her.

May 26, 1907
Future movie idol John Wayne is born Marion Morrison in Winterset, Iowa.

1908
First Mother's Day is observed.

February 29, 1908
Pat Garrett is murdered near Las Cruces, New Mexico. Although Wayne Brazel, a 21-year-old cowboy, confessed to the killings, some historians believe the deed was done by hired assassin Jim Miller.

October 1, 1908
Henry Ford launches his Model T automobile, priced at $850.

November 4, 1908
Butch Cassidy and the Sundance Kid rob the Aramayo, Francke & Co. payroll in Southern Bolivia.

November 6, 1908
Trapped by a posse in San Vicente in the Bolivian Andes, Butch Cassidy supposedly shoots the Sundance Kid and then kills himself.

1909
The National Association for the

13 ♦ As a counteroffensive to Huerta's regime, the military commanders of Chihuahua and Durango elected Villa on September 26, 1913, to command a formidable army known as the Division del Norte (later called the Villistas) and attack government-controlled Torreon. After Villa captured Torreon, Ciudad Juarez and Tierra Blanca, he was elected military governor of Chihuahua.

14 ♦ In 1914, the left-wing American journalist John Reed (the subject of the 1981 movie *Reds*, starring Warren Beatty) traveled with Villa's army and came to admire the general. Reed's book *Insurgent Mexico* was based on his experiences with Villa and his men.

15 ♦ John Reed dubbed Villa the "Mexican Robin Hood." Villa also acquired the nickname "Lion of the North."

16 ♦ As military governor of Chihuahua, Villa was generous to the poor. He used stolen money to help widows and orphans, build schools, fund pensions, electrify the city and care for soldiers' families.

17 ♦ Four months after he was elected governor, Villa resigned and appointed Manuel Chao.

18 ♦ Villa was a notorious womanizer and in his heyday had a "wife" in towns across Northern Mexico. His first wife Luz Corral said in her memoirs: "for a housewife, the love affairs of her husband should be of no importance as long as the wife is loved and respected in her home, which is her sanctuary."

19 ♦ Noting that Villa neither smoked nor drank, an American journalist asked the general if he had any redeeming vices. "Women," replied the Lion of the North, "I am a son of a bitch when it comes to women."

20 ♦ Villa's military success and popularity with the Mexican peasantry peaked in 1914, the same year the silent film *The Life of General Villa* was released. Hollywood bankrolled Pancho's army in exchange for being allowed to film him in battle, which is the premise of the 2003 HBO movie *And Starring Pancho Villa as Himself*.

Apache Chief Goyathlay or Geronimo.

Advancement of Colored People (NAACP) is founded in New York City.

February 17, 1909
Geronimo dies at Fort Sill, Oklahoma, around the age of 80.

1910
Government officials prohibit the Plains Indians from performing the Sun Dance.

February 8, 1910
Boy Scouts of America founded.

October 1, 1910
Bonnie Parker (of Bonnie & Clyde) is born in Rowena, Texas.

November 8, 1910
Iowa schoolteacher Jessie Shambaugh starts the first 4-H Club. (The 4-H's stand for Heads, Hands, Heart and Health.)

February 10, 1911
Zerelda James, Frank and Jesse's mother, passes away at age 86.

May 15, 1911
The U.S. Supreme Court breaks up John D. Rockefeller's Standard Oil Company.

Sept. 17–Nov. 5, 1911
C.P. Rodgers makes the first successful transcontinental airplane flight, going from New York to Pasadena, California (total air time: 82 hours, four minutes).

1912
Zane Grey's *Riders of the Purple Sage* is published. The first Girl Scout troop is established by Juliette Gordon Low of Savannah, Georgia. Sauk Indian Jim Thorpe wins medals at the Olympic Games in Stockholm, Sweden.

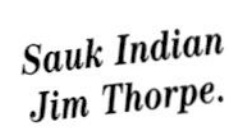

Sauk Indian Jim Thorpe.

On December 6, 1914, Pancho Villa entered Mexico City in full military uniform, which may be the costume Hollywood had him wear in the film The Life of General Villa. *From left to right, behind buglers is ex-President of Mexico Gen. Abelardo L. Rodriguez, Gen. Tomas Urbina, Gen. Emiliano Zapata (wearing a sombrero), Gen. Pancho Villa and Villa's infamous "butcherer" Rodolfo Fierro. Whereas Villa commanded revolutionary forces in Northern Mexico, Zapata commanded those in the South. To show his good faith, Villa once choked down a large glass of cognac Zapata offered him even though he usually didn't drink alcohol. In 1919, Zapata was assassinated. Pancho suffered the same fate in 1923.*

BUILDING THE AMERICAN WEST

March 13, 1912
Ben Kilpatrick—the last active member of the Wild Bunch—is bludgeoned to death by a Wells Fargo messenger during a failed train holdup near Sanderson, Texas. (Elzy Lay lives until 1934; Matt Warner until 1938; Walt Puteney until 1950. Last to die was Kilpatrick's girlfriend, Laura Bullion, in 1961.)

Titanic *sinks on maiden voyage.*

April 14, 1912
The passenger liner *Titanic* sinks on its maiden voyage after striking an iceberg in the North Atlantic.

1913
The "Buffalo Head" nickel is introduced. Indian Jim Thorpe is stripped of his Olympic medals because he played semi-professional baseball. (In 1982, Thorpe regained his standing as a two-time Olympic gold medalist 30 years after his death.)

April 29, 1913
Gideon Sundback patents his separable fastener, better known as the zipper.

January 5, 1914
Ford Motor Company raises the minimum wage from $2.40 for a nine-hour day to $5 for an eight-hour day.

March 18, 1914
Joe Small, founder of *True West* magazine, is born.

True West *magazine founder, Joe Austin Small.*

June 28, 1914
In Sarajevo, Bosnia, Austria's Archduke Ferdinand is assassinated, plunging Europe into the Great War (a.k.a. WW I).

August 15, 1914
Panama Canal officially opens.

February 8, 1915
D.W. Griffith's film *Birth of a Nation* premieres in Los Angeles. The movie introduces the close-up, the panoramic shot, the flashback and the use of a moving camera.

February 18, 1915
Frank James dies at home in Missouri.

21 ♦ Pancho usually carried a Colt Single Action Army revolver.

22 ♦ Pancho's favorite rifle was a Winchester Model 1895.

23 ♦ Pancho Villa loved to be photographed—more photos were taken of the charismatic general than of any other field commander during the Mexican Revolution.

24 ♦ Villa's official photographer was an American from El Paso named Otis Aultman, who Villa nicknamed the "Banty Rooster." The *gringo* traveled with the general to document his triumphs.

25 ♦ Villa's speech was peppered with unprintable phrases. In spite of this, Villa became a favorite with the American press.

26 ♦ Villa could be brutal as a commander and often sent prisoners to the firing squad.

General Emiliano Zapata

Austria's Archduke and his wife.

April 22, 1915
German soldiers unleash a new weapon: poison gas.

May 7, 1915
German submarine sinks the British passenger liner *Lusitania*, killing 128 Americans.

March 9, 1916
Mexican troops led by Pancho Villa raid Columbus, New Mexico. Later in the year, American soldiers commanded by Gen. John J. Pershing invade Mexico in pursuit of Pancho Villa.

***A single torpedo sinks* Lusitania.**

1917
Nellie T. Ross of Wyoming is the nation's first elected female governor.

February 1, 1917
Arizona's Papago Indian Reservation becomes the last reservation established by executive order.

January 10, 1917
Buffalo Bill Cody dies in Denver, Colorado, at age 70.

April 6, 1917
U.S. declares war on Germany, officially entering WW I.

27 ♦ In April 1915, forces under the command of Gen. Alvaro Obregon (chief military commander under Venustiano Carranza, the Constitutionalist governor of Coahuila) decisively defeated Villa's army at Celaya. The Villistas never regained their importance as a fighting force.

28 ♦ On October 19, 1915, President Woodrow Wilson's administration recognized Carranza's regime as the lawful government of Mexico. Carranza and Villa were bitter enemies, so Wilson's decision enraged Villa, who vowed to punish the Americans.

29 ♦ On March 9, 1916, some 485 Villistas raided Columbus, New Mexico, and the small army post on the outskirts of town. During the fracas, 18 Americans and over 100 Mexicans were killed. The raid began about 4 A.M., while it was still dark, and was over in about two hours.

30 ♦ Several townspeople swore they recognized Villa among the men who terrorized Columbus, however, a captured Villista later wrote that the general stayed behind with a rear guard and did not enter the town with his raiders.

The Feminine Brigade in Mexico City. After the Mexican Revolution,* soldaderas *were reduced to a legend in one* corrido *(folk song) that refers to Adelita, who followed the troops in battle because she was madly in love with her sergeant. Some other* corridos *about* soldaderas *also distorted the true roles these courageous women played.

Gen. Smedley Butler hacks away for prohibition in Philadelphia.

BUILDING THE AMERICAN WEST

November 11, 1918
WW I ends with the surrender of Germany and her allies. That year an influenza epidemic erupted, eventually killing about 20 million people worldwide.

1919
Rotary dial telephones are introduced.

January 16, 1919
The 18th Amendment becomes law: prohibition begins.

February 26, 1919
The Grand Canyon is set aside as a national park.

May 8–27, 1919
U.S. Navy seaplane makes the first transatlantic flight, from Rockaway, New York, to Lisbon, Portugal.

August 18, 1920
The 19th Amendment is ratified, allowing women to vote.

August 20, 1920
First licensed radio broadcast.

The National Woman's Party celebrates the right to vote.

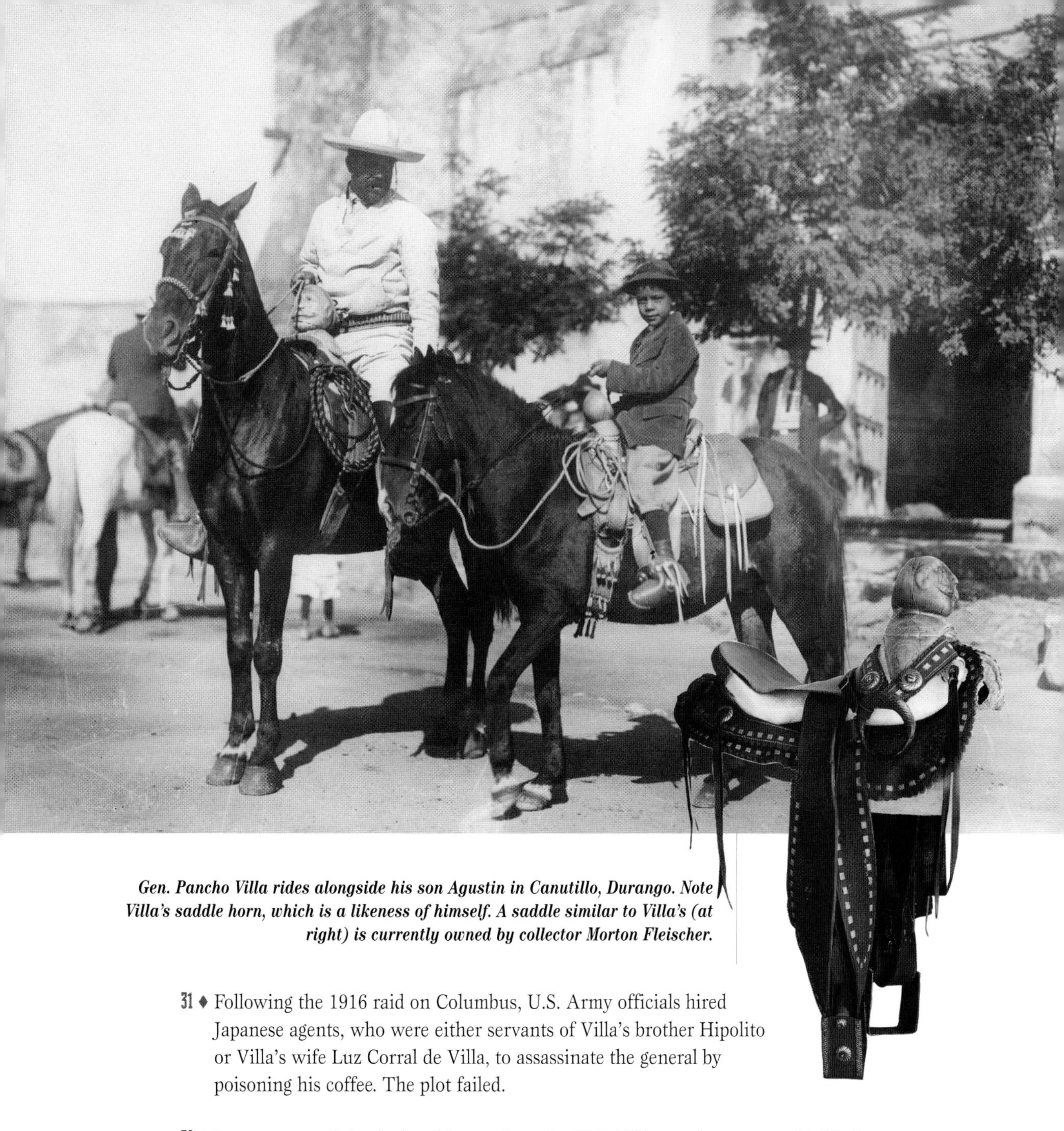

Gen. Pancho Villa rides alongside his son Agustin in Canutillo, Durango. Note Villa's saddle horn, which is a likeness of himself. A saddle similar to Villa's (at right) is currently owned by collector Morton Fleischer.

31 ♦ Following the 1916 raid on Columbus, U.S. Army officials hired Japanese agents, who were either servants of Villa's brother Hipolito or Villa's wife Luz Corral de Villa, to assassinate the general by poisoning his coffee. The plot failed.

32 ♦ It was rumored that before his attack on the U.S., Villa was in contact with his former munitions buyer Felix Sommerfeld, who had joined the German Secret Service in 1915. The Kaiser hoped a war between Mexico and the U.S. would keep America out of the war in Europe.

Assassins murdered Pancho Villa (right) on July 20, 1923, three years after the end of the Mexican Revolution.

33 ♦ Because of Villa's raid, the U.S. Army brought eight of its 13 airplanes to Columbus, making it the first wartime U.S. air base.

34 ♦ The American military incursion into Mexico (organized to kill or capture Villa) lasted about 10 months. Although a few skirmishes were fought, Villa escaped Gen. John Pershing's nearly 10,000-man force unscathed.

35 ♦ One of the officers involved in the 1916 American expedition into Mexico was Lt. George S. Patton, Jr. (of WW II fame).

36 ♦ After the close of the open warfare phase of the Mexican Revolution in 1920, the Mexican government awarded Villa a large hacienda with 50 men for protection, land for his soldiers and a military pension for all. The former *peon* became a wealthy man.

37 ♦ On July 20, 1923, Pancho was driving an open-top Dodge touring car near Parral, Chihuahua, when he was gunned down by his political enemies in Bonnie and Clyde style. Pancho was 45 years old.

38 ♦ After Pancho's death, his first of several wives, Senora Luz Corral, reportedly kept a holstered revolver in plain sight in her Chihuahua City home, the Quinta Luz. Visitors to the residence often inquired about the gun. Luz told them it had been Pancho's and would ask if the visitor wanted to buy it. When the caller left with his prize, she'd get another gun out of a drawer and put it in the holster. A local gunsmith kept her supplied with revolvers, and she made good money selling them.

39 ♦ For many years, Luz Corral kept her dead husband's bullet-ridden Dodge car at her home in Chihuahua City. Tourists came from afar to view the grisly auto. She died in 1981.

40 ♦ The Villa home in Chihuahua City is a museum, now owned by the Mexican Army and is called the *Museo de la Revolucion* (Museum of the Revolution). This 50-room mansion is filled with Pancho Villa's mementos and furniture.

41 ♦ A 1932 rumor circulated that Pancho's grave had been opened and his head stolen. Reportedly, phrenologists (crackpot "scientists" who studied the bumps on skulls) at the University of Chicago paid $10,000 for it.

42 ♦ In the late 1980s, stories about Pancho's skull again surfaced, this time in regard to President George Bush's old fraternity at Yale: the Skull and Bones Society. Pancho's skull was thought to be a treasured relic used in the Society's secret ceremonies. Spokesmen for Skull and Bones denied possessing the artifact.

43 ♦ The 1934 hit Hollywood film *Viva Villa!* starring Wallace Beery was loosely based on Pancho's exploits as a military leader.

44 ♦ The Mexican Government presented Tucson, Arizona, with a 14-foot bronze statue of Pancho Villa astride a rearing horse, which was erected in 1981. There was some dismay but more amusement at the irony of the gift, which, after much discussion, was accepted. The statue stands in downtown Tucson.

45 ♦ For several years after the statue of Villa was erected in Tucson, every March 9 an outraged citizen placed small white crosses at the base of the monument in recognition of the Americans killed by Villa's forces during the Columbus, New Mexico, raid.

46 ♦ Although a statue of Gen. Villa stands proudly in Tucson, there is no statue of Gen. John "Black Jack" Pershing on display in Mexico.

Gen. Francisco "Pancho" Villa with his first wife, Luz Corral de Villa. After Pancho's death, Senora Luz Corral turned the mansion she had shared with him into a museum.

47 ♦ In 1983, Willie Nelson recorded a song titled "Pancho & Lefty." Of course, the "Pancho" was Pancho Villa.

48 ♦ Pancho Villa remains a hero in Mexico, particularly among the poor. But among some Chihuahuan descendants of aristocratic land owners, he is regarded as a ruthless outlaw.

49 ♦ Ironically, Pancho Villa is the biggest asset the little town of Columbus, New Mexico, has today. Tourists come to see the place where a foreign army attacked the United States, which brings the town much-needed dollars. Pancho Villa State Park provides camping sites and interpretive displays. A grease rack used to lubricate U.S. Army vehicles during the punitive incursion into Mexico is proudly featured.

50 ♦ With a state park named for Pancho Villa in New Mexico and a majestic statue of the Lion of the North in Arizona, the Mexican bandit-general continues to make his presence felt north of the border.

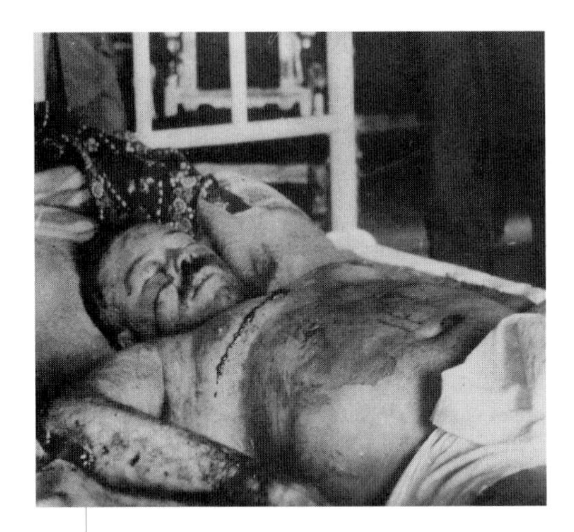

After a lookout cried "Viva Villa," assassins on horseback fired nine bullets into Villa, killing him instantly.

RAID ON COLUMBUS

AMERICA ATTACKED

ON *September 11, 2001, terrorists invaded the United States and killed Americans on our own soil. The nation grieves to this day.*

THIS WAS NOT THE FIRST TIME FOREIGN AGGRESSORS CROSSED OUR BORDERS and spilled American blood. On March 9, 1916, around 485 Mexican troops commanded by Francisco "Pancho" Villa attacked Columbus, New Mexico, and took American lives. That assault was the closing chapter in the history of the Old West.

Colonel Frank Tompkins, at the time a major in the U.S. Cavalry and second in command of the 266-man army garrison in Columbus, Lt. John P. Lucas and Sgt. Michael Fody saw the fight firsthand. Their words, taken from Tompkins' 1934 book, *Chasing Villa*, give a chilling account of a town under fire.

LIEUTENANT LUCAS

The town of Columbus . . . did not present an attractive appearance. A cluster of adobe houses, a hotel, a few stores and streets knee-deep in sand, combined with the cactus, mesquite and rattlesnakes. . . . Life at Columbus was not exciting. There was little to do and plenty of time to do it in. As I look back on it, however, I forget the sand storms, the heat and the monotony of existence in this sun-baked, little desert town. I forget the habit of the rattlers to occupy our houses. I forget also the fact that the nearest tree was in El Paso, 75 miles away. I remember only the pride with which I commanded my troop.

MAJOR TOMPKINS

On the afternoon of March 7th I patrolled about 15 miles east of the border gate. Close to midnight . . . I accompanied Col. Slocum [commander of American forces at Columbus] to the border gate to interview the commanding officer of the Carranzista troops [Mexican soldiers loyal to Villa's rival, Venustiano Carranza] stationed there. When these soldiers heard our horses approaching, they sprang to arms and took shelter designed to offer protection from attack from the direction of the United States. Their conduct showed all the symptoms of a guilty conscience. I believed then and I believe now they were aware of Villa's movements and intentions and I am convinced some of them took part in the attack.

The Mexicans [Villa's troops] crossed the international boundary line at a point about three miles west of the border gate. They sifted across in small bands, united at a point safe from observation from our patrols, then marched northeast until within about one half mile of the American camp when they split into two attacking columns. The first column moved to the south of the camp, then east and attacked the stables from a southeasterly direction. The second column crossed the drainage ditch immediately west of the camp at the custom house, where they divided, the first half attacking the camp from the west and the second half moving into the town where they proceeded to loot, murder and burn.

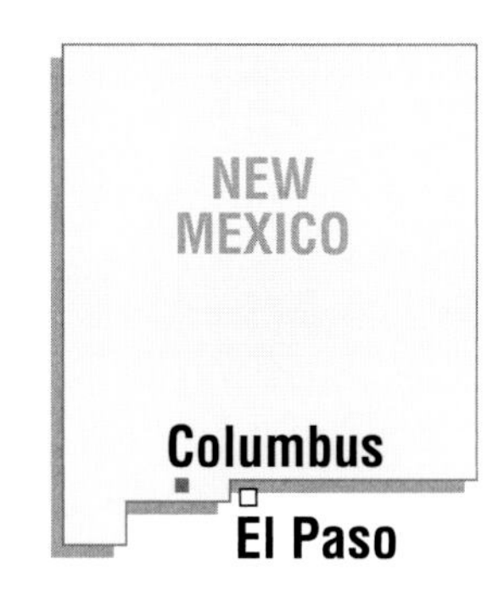

Private Fred Griffin, Troop K, 13th Cavalry, was the first man killed in the fight. Griffin was a sentinel on post No. 3, around the regimental headquarters, so he was nearest to the

Mexican revolutionaries slipped into Columbus, New Mexico, on March 9, 1916.

first point of attack by the Mexicans. He challenged a Mexican who answered by shooting the sentinel, but Griffin killed this Mexican and two others before he died.

Private John D. Yarborough, sentinel on post No. 1 at the guard house, was very badly wounded in the right arm when that side of the camp was attacked, but he fought through the entire action with his arm hanging useless.

SERGEANT FODY

[Hearing the firing, Sgt. Michael Fody headed toward it with F Troop.]

Just as we cleared the width of the barracks to the lane leading towards headquarters, Lt. James Castleman came running to me with his revolver in his hand and took command of the troop. We proceeded towards headquarters and after advancing about 200 yards we encountered a heavy fire, so close that the flash almost scorched our faces. Instantly every man in the troop dropped to the ground and opened fire. On account of the darkness it was impossible to distinguish anyone, and for the moment I was under the impression that we were being fired on by some of our own regiment who had preceded us to the scene. The feeling was indescribable, and when I heard the Mexican voices opposite us you can imagine my relief. As soon as there was a lull in the fighting, Lt. Castleman ordered the troop on towards the town, where the heaviest firing was concentrated.

LIEUTENANT LUCAS

About 4:30 A.M. I was awakened by someone riding by the open window of my room. I looked out, and although the night was very dark, I saw a man wearing a black sombrero riding towards camp. From the sounds I heard, it seemed to me he had quite a few companions and that the house was completely surrounded. I knew who they were because

Following Villa's raid, Columbus civilians evacuated their town and walked to a waiting train.

Villa's officers affected the type of headgear I had noticed. We heard later that this party was composed of Villa himself and 35 or 40 of his officers. They were the only ones who approached on horseback.

I got hold of my gun and stationed myself in the middle of the room where I could command the door, determined to get a few of them before they got me. I was saved, however, by a member of the guard, and I have always felt that I owed him a great debt of gratitude. Unfortunately, he was killed. This soldier [Pvt. Griffin] was posted at regimental headquarters, which was within sight of my house. He evidently saw the Mexicans approaching because he opened fire on them and they immediately left my house and charged him. They galloped right on through camp and down to the stables which were 400 or 500 yards east of the barracks.

When the Mexicans left my house, I was able to get out and follow them on into camp to turn out my men. In the dark I was unable to find my boots so that I was forced to go barefooted for about an hour and a half and had very little skin left on the soles of my feet. It took me over six months to get all of the sand burrs out. The sentinel who had saved my life had gotten one Mexican but had been shot through the belly and was dying when I went by.

I reached my barracks and told the acting first sergeant to turn out the men and follow me down to the guard tent. The guard tent was near the stables and standing order required that we keep the machine guns under lock and key in the guard tent as they could be sold to the Mexicans for $500 or $600 apiece. Without waiting for my troop I took two men, a corporal and the horseshoer, and proceeded immediately to the guard tent. My idea was to get a gun out and in action to keep the Mexicans out of camp. By this time the town was full of them.

So far I had seen no other officers. All those who lived in the town, and a majority of them did, had been surrounded in their houses and had been unable to get out. Two officers, Lt. Stringfellow and myself, lived in camp, and were the only ones present in the first phase of the conflict. . . . The officer of the day was required to sleep in a small adobe house in the center of camp. I had looked into this house as I passed and had seen that it was empty. Lieutenant James Castleman was officer of the day and . . . he had turned out his troop—I have forgotten which one he commanded—and marched it over to town, where he took station in front of his residence and opposite the bank.

The Mexicans were poor shots and to this fact we certainly owed our light casualty list. One of them fired at me with a rifle while I was on my way to the guard tent. He missed me even though he was so close that I easily killed him with a revolver and I was never noted for my excellence in pistol practice.

We reached the guard tent and got out one of the guns. The sentinel on post No. 1 [Pvt. Yarborough] was lying across the door of the tent. He died later. The three of us set the gun up where we could command one of the crossings over the railroad. It was very dark but we could see the flash of the Mexican rifles. They burned up thousands of rounds of ammunition. As I remember the affair, the corporal acted as gunner while I loaded the piece. The gun was the old Benèt-Mercier . . . which required perfect conditions in order that it might function. The conditions not being perfect the gun jammed after a few rounds, and we left it in position and went after another. The corporal's remarks were enlightening but not printable. The jam was reduced later and the gun returned to action.

By this time, the remainder of the troop had arrived and I stationed the guns in what I considered to be strategic positions to fire on the Mexicans in town. Also about 30 men with rifles had shown up, and these I deployed along the railroad track to fire on the same target. Lieutenant Stringfellow also came up about that time, and, being senior to him, I sent him with some men to protect our left flank from any further invasion from the west.

This may sound like an account of "Alone at Columbus," but, as a matter of fact, none of the officers who were marooned in town were able to get to camp until our fire had cleared up the situation to some extent. About the time I got my "army" nicely deployed the Mexicans set fire to the hotel in town. This lit up the terrain so effectively that we were able to see our targets very plainly. Also, Castleman's move to town with his troop proved to be strategically correct as it enabled us to bring a cross-fire on the enemy. The Mexicans stood it for a few minutes only, when they commenced to fall back. Captain Hamilton Bowie was the first officer to be released and he immediately came into camp.

I turned over my command to Capt. Bowie, and, taking a few men with me, worked around the enemy left into town. My idea was to clear the town and do what I could to protect the families of our officers from the Mexicans. To my surprise I found Castleman and his men there already. I had no idea of his whereabouts before. It was just about daylight when I joined Castleman and a few minutes later the colonel appeared. I then returned to

WHY PANCHO VILLA ATTACKED

The previous year, the United States recognized the regime of Venustiano Carranza, Villa's bitter enemy, as the legitimate government of Mexico. Later, Carranza's forces were allowed to use U.S. railroads to move troops into position to fight Villa's ragtag army. Pancho Villa, an impulsive man of action, wanted to punish the Americans for siding with his opponents.

camp and, after daylight, was sent by the colonel with 15 or 20 men to relieve Capt. Stedje at the gate and allow his troops to pursue the enemy who were, by this time, in full retreat.

MAJOR FRANK TOMPKINS

The kitchen shacks of the camp were of adobe construction, erected by the troops and bullet proof. The desert around Columbus was full of rabbits and quail. It was customary for each troop to keep in the kitchen a company shotgun with ammunition. This enabled one of the kitchen crew to go out in the afternoon and bring back a mess of quail or rabbits. When the Mexicans made their attack, the unexpected resistance they met broke them up into small groups. The fire of the American soldiers was so hot and accurate that these small groups sought shelter behind the bullet proof kitchen shacks. The kitchen crews could hear them talking outside the kitchen windows—so they promptly fired into them with the shotguns. Those of the Mexicans who were not killed by this fire took back into Mexico some American shot under their hides.

One group of Mexicans broke in the door of a kitchen shack. The crew were waiting for them: one cook soused them with boiling water while the other cook sailed into them with an axe. When the smoke of battle cleared the only Mexicans left on that particular spot were dead Mexicans.

Another group [of Mexicans] took shelter against a kitchen wall. They were located by one of the machine guns. The gun crew gave them a burst of fire at short range, firing low to get advantage of ricochets. Few of that party of Mexicans ever saw Mexico again. They were literally cut to pieces by these ricocheting bullets. On my return from the pursuit I took a look at this place and saw several pieces of human skull as large as my hand, with the long hair of the Yaqui Indian attached.

One soldier of the stable crew killed a Mexican with a baseball bat. As a matter of fact the Mexicans were getting it from all sides. In the darkness and confusion some [of our] soldiers became separated from their troops. These men carried on a private war of their own, shooting Mexicans whenever they saw one or more. This reception was so totally different from what they [Villa's troops] had been told to expect that the camp and the town too, was soon cleared of the enemy.

Captain Rudolph E. Smyser, with his wife and two children, occupied a house on the western edge of town across the street from my quarters. The Mexicans battered in their front door as Smyser and his family climbed out of a back window and took refuge in an outhouse. They heard the Mexicans talking of searching the place, so Smyser and family abandoned the outhouse for the mesquite and got pretty well filled with cactus thorns.

Lieutenant William A. McCain lived with his wife and little girl in a house near the southwest edge of the town, not far from the railroad track. In the first moments of the attack this house was surrounded by a swarm of Mexicans. In the building . . . in addition to the family, was . . . McCain's orderly. As soon as the first Mexican wave passed, the McCain party evacuated the house, moved south across the railroad tracks, and hid in the mesquite.

[As the Mexicans fell back, they] passed all around the bush under which the McCain party were hiding. Captain George Williams, the regimental adjutant, who had been cut off from camp, stumbled into McCain at this moment. McCain and his orderly had between them a pistol and a shotgun. Captain Williams had his pistol. It was still dark. The retreating Mexicans were thinning out; falling back in small groups, in pairs, and singly. They would halt, fire towards the camp and then continue to retreat. Finally, an isolated Mexican discovered the Americans. Before he could give the alarm, Lt. McCain shot him with the shotgun but did not kill him. They pulled him under a bush. He struggled and tried to give the alarm. McCain did not want to shoot him again for fear that the shot might betray their hiding place. Something had to be done to silence the cries of the wounded Mexican. They tried to cut his throat with a pocket knife but the knife was too dull. They finally killed him by hammering in his head with the butt of a pistol.

Realizing that the Mexicans were whipped, I [Maj. Tompkins] asked Col. Slocum to allow me to mount up a troop and take the offensive. He authorized me to take Troop H, commanded by Capt. Rudolph Smyser. In about 20 minutes we managed to mount 32 men and left camp. We proceeded southwest, and in the dim light of early morning saw the

This photo of the "Home Guard" of Columbus was taken shortly before Villa's raid. These civilians, mostly ranchers from the area, were deputized as U.S. marshals or assistants.

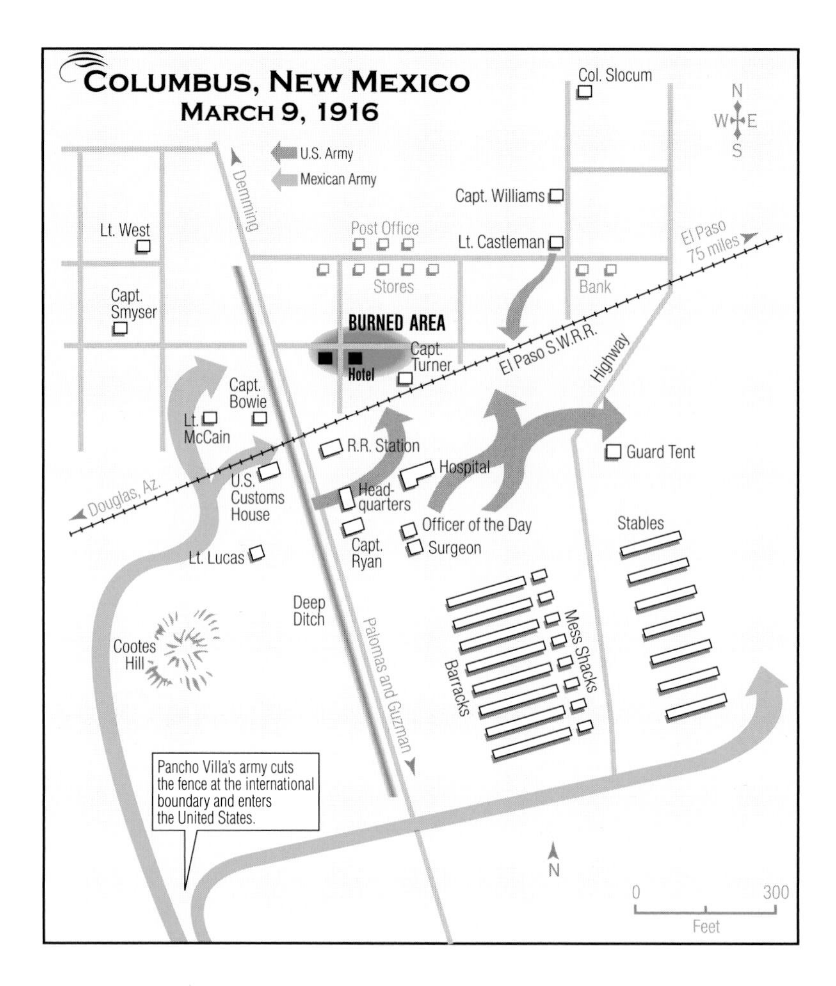

Mexican column retreating south towards the border. We paralleled their march with the object of cutting off as many as possible as soon as we could get clear of the wire fences. We finally reached the border fence with the loss of one horse killed.

There was an isolated hill about 300 yards south of the fence between the Mexican column and my forces. This hill was occupied by Mexican troops. [The Americans charged.]

The fire of the enemy went high, but they held on until we hit the lower slopes of the hill when they broke and ran. We galloped to the hilltop . . . dismounted, and opened fire with rifles on the fleeing Mexicans, killing 32 men and many horses.

[Realizing he was in Mexico, Maj. Tompkins requested reinforcements from Columbus. After they arrived, he continued the pursuit south of the border and hit Villa's rear guard.]

We deployed at wide intervals and advanced towards the enemy at a fast trot, the enemy firing all the time but their shots going wild. When we were within 400 yards of them . . . we dismounted, and opened fire, driving the rear guard back on the main body and killing and wounding quite a few.

We again took up the pursuit, and in about 30 minutes overtook the rear guard. I received a slight wound in the knee, a bullet through the rim of my hat, and my horse was wounded slightly in the head.

[After the Mexicans were again driven back, Maj. Tompkins' troops continued to dog their heels.] I again overtook the enemy, but this time on a plain devoid of cover. They soon saw our weakness (but 29 men) and started an attack with at least 300 men, while the remainder of the Mexican forces continued their retreat. We returned their fire until one horse was wounded and one killed when we fell back about 400 yards where our horses had excellent cover. But the Mexicans refused to advance against us in this new position.

After waiting about 45 minutes I returned to Columbus . . . having been gone seven and one half hours, covered 30 miles of rough country, fought four separate rear guard actions without the loss of a single man, and inflicted a loss of from 75 to 100 killed.

"Villa, 'The Lion of the North,' was not only defeated at Columbus, but he at once became a fugitive from American justice, and was chased by American troops for over 500 miles through his native country at terrific cost to his prestige and power. The fight at Columbus caused his star to wane, and it so continued until he was assassinated on the outskirts of Parral in 1923."

TRUTH FAILED TO HIDE IN A TIN

A HIDDEN GUN HELPS SOLVE AN OLD WEST MURDER

WHEN *his hired hand stomped off in a huff that chilled November day in 1895, foreman Jim Potts knew it would be up to him to take care of his band of sheep.*

POTTS HEADED TO THEIR GRAZING SPOT NEAR THE NORTH FORK of the Powder River, just north of Kaycee, Wyoming. He watched his "woolies" work their way south across the range that had been recently brushed with a thin sheet of new snow, before he trudged toward three large sandstone buttes. From there, he thought he could best keep an eye on his flock.

As he made his way to the north side of the buttes, he found a large piece of caprock had split off. He spotted a space—about eight or ten inches deep—that someone had neatly filled with small stones. As he plucked out the pebbles, he saw what looked like a rectangular piece of bright metal. At first, he thought it to be a gold brick, rumored to have been stolen in Nevada some months before and then cached here in Johnson County. But as Potts dug deeper, he instead found a five-pound Prices Baking Powder can with a loose lid.

As he removed the tin, a bright-skinned, nearly new, nickel-plated, .45 caliber Colt revolver fell out. It had a lanyard swivel on the butt of its pearl-handled grip. From inside the tin, Potts pulled out a fistful of papers that had been shredded by varmints. Disappointed that he hadn't found gold, Potts pocketed the handgun and went back to watching his sheep. He had no idea his discovery would one day help solve a notorious murder.

FOUR DECADES LATER

The revolver stayed in a bureau drawer at Potts' home for the next four decades, with few people, other than the family, knowing of its existence. Then in 1938, "Black Billy" Hill, a small-time rancher of questionable character, returned from Canada to visit. Johnson County Sheriff Martin A. "Mart" Tisdale took Hill, his deceased father's one-time friend, to visit his old ranch site.

According to the sheriff, Hill pointed to three isolated sandstone buttes that rose sharply from the plains and dropped a bombshell. It was there, Hill claimed, that notorious Red Sash Gang member Ed Starr said he had buried a gun and papers he took from U.S. Deputy Marshal George A. Wellman—after he had killed him.

This model 1878 Colt .45 caliber revolver was stolen from the body of U.S. Deputy Marshal George A. Wellman after he was shot and killed by an assassin in Johnson County, Wyoming. The double-action pistol has serial number 10373, indicating it was manufactured in Hartford, Connecticut, in 1883.

During the infamous Johnson County War, George A. Wellman was secretly enlisted as a U.S. deputy marshal to "assemble evidence to prove that the homes, ranches and herds of the stockmen were being looted and rustled." On May 9, 1892, he was en route to Buffalo, Wyoming, when an assassin shot and killed him.

When the lawman returned later that day to the Johnson County Courthouse in Buffalo, Wyoming, he told Hill's tale about the cached gun to an astonished Warren Lott. Lott's boss was County Treasurer J.W. "Joe" Potts, whose father was Jim Potts. Upon hearing the story, Joe told how and where his father had found a Colt revolver 43 years earlier.

When ex-Buffalo Mayor C.H. Burritt learned of the story, he had Thomas "Tommy" F. Carr, a one-time mail carrier in the area, and famed lawman Joe LeFors examine the weapon. Both confirmed that the gun had belonged to Marshal Wellman and that they had seen the sidearm many times on his hip. Burritt also asked Lora "Lorry" H. Reed—a billiard parlor operator—if he recognized the pistol. "That's it!" exclaimed Reed, who just before the murder had been one of Wellman's ranch hands. Reed assured the mayor that he not only remembered the gun but even recalled a "circle on the left side" of its grip, which Burritt confirmed to be true. Not having a gun of his own at the time, Reed remembered that his admiration of the revolver was so great, "every chance he got, he would examine and fondle" it.

More than four decades after the pistol had been found by chance in the tin—Hill's casual aside would help solve one of the most mysterious murders in Old West history.

AMBUSHED

George A. Wellman, a Canadian by birth, had hired on at the HOE Ranch and became its foreman in 1887. From that vantage point, he watched the growing bloodshed between ranchers and rustlers that became the Johnson County range war.

Wellman apparently bought his beloved Colt around July 20, 1889, after "Cattle Kate" Watson and her lover Jim Averell were hanged near Independence Rock, Wyoming, on suspicion of brand-running.

Their deaths began a series of murders and attempted murders among cow thieves and ranchers. On June 4, 1891, a group of thugs—presumably backed by ranchers—posed as lawmen and took Tom Waggoner, a reputed horse thief, from his home. Folks soon found Waggoner decorating a cottonwood branch near Newcastle, Wyoming. Five months later, on the Powder River, Nate Champion, another suspected cow thief, was almost murdered. That same month, assassins hid beneath a bridge some 15 miles south of Buffalo, and as 23-year-old Orley E. "Ranger" Jones rode by, they shot him to death. Soon thereafter, some seven miles north of where Jones had died, assassins left rancher John A. Tisdale stone-dead. Friends found the corpse of Mart Tisdale's dad in a pile of Christmas toys and supplies the old man had planned to take home to his family. By April 10, 1892, such depredations by both sides finally exploded into a full-scale war that raged for three days.

"[Johnson County is] a good place for fugitives from justice," Wellman once said. "There are more desperate criminals there than probably could be found in any place on earth. These men lead a riotous life. They are notorious gamblers, thieves and murderers, and none of them ever think of working for a living. The rough country enables them to carry on their depredations with a free hand. They steal unbranded and stray cattle—branded cattle, too, sometimes—and in that way they have been getting rich at the expense of the cattle owners. There has always been trouble between the two parties."

The cattlemen had tried time and time again to have these outlaws punished, but no matter how strong the evidence against them, it was impossible to secure conviction as the juries almost always decided against the cattlemen. The ranchers finally resolved to take the law into their own hands.

Accordingly, it's understandable why soon after Wellman went back East to wed Lucy C. Clark on April 21, he insured his life. It seems he also planned to quit the West, as he left his wife behind and told his family he intended to close up his affairs and move to Bay City, Michigan.

"Black Billy" Hill was a small-time rancher of questionable character who fled to Canada during the Johnson County War. In 1938, he returned to Wyoming and told Sheriff "Mart" Tisdale that a thug by the name of Ed Starr had buried "the gun and papers he took off of Wellman" after Starr murdered Wellman. Starr was a member of the Red Sash Gang. The members were recognized by the red strips of cloth worn beneath their gun belts.

Soon after his return to Wyoming, Wellman teamed up with rancher Robert Lee Gibson, and they secretly swore oaths as U.S. deputy marshals to help stop the lawlessness. Presumably, Wellman's instructions were to "assemble evidence to prove that the homes, ranches and herds of the stockmen were being looted and rustled." That evidence would be sent to Washington, D.C. and, it was hoped, would persuade President Benjamin Harrison to declare martial law in Johnson County.

The orders Wellman received were simple and to the point, and they may have worked, had he and Gibson not discussed them in a crowded bar. Armed with his secret assignment, Wellman returned to his ranch, paid his wranglers and fired several suspected thieves, including Austin Reed and his 19-year-old brother Lorry.

On the night of May 8, Wellman prepared for his trip back to Buffalo, taking along his prized pistol. He left the next morning with Thomas J. "Big Mouth" Hathaway, a 36-year-old ranch employee.

The two were approaching Nine Mile Divide when they heard shots. Hathaway later reported: "Well, I and Mr. Wellman was riding side by side . . . talking and the first thing I knew I heard a couple of shots just very quick right together like; made my horse jump so did Mr. Wellmans . . . and as I pulled up my horse I faced him [Wellman] and he threw up one hand and hollo'd; he did not hollo as though he was hurt, he hollo'd like he was trying to hale somebody or simply as a man would hollo 'hey' at somebody and at that time there was two more shots fired right after that so close that I could not tell, and I started my horse on the run and got away from there."

All that remains of the large HOE Ranch is this double-stone chimney, which was built to heat two rooms from adjoining sides. The ranch was situated on the Powder River, 50 miles southeast of Buffalo, Wyoming, and was owned by Henry A. Blair, a wealthy man from Chicago. Wellman worked as ranch foreman from 1887 until his mysterious death in 1892.

U.S. Marshal Joseph P. Rankin wanted President Benjamin Harrison to declare martial law in Johnson County, so he recruited Wellman to secretly serve as his deputy. Rankin was to report any alarming findings to the U.S. attorney in Cheyenne, Wyoming, who would pass the information on to Washington, D.C.

Hathaway said he did not return to Wellman's body, because he "was entirely unarmed."

What Hathaway did not know is that soon after Wellman hit the ground, someone stole the lawman's pistol from his still warm body and rushed it from the scene.

RED SASH BOYS

It would take years for anyone to piece together what had happened. A decade after the killing, Mayor Burritt told of a ride he had with fellow herder Austin Reed, around 1892. Reed admitted he was present when members of the Red Sash Gang drew lots to determine who would kill Wellman. "It had been framed for Ed Starr to draw that ticket," Reed noted. "Starr was a killer and would as soon shoot a man as a coyote." He added that he "had often heard Starr imitate Wellman's cry when he saw he was going to be killed."

But perhaps the most damning evidence came from the mail carrier Tommy Carr, who said he had stayed at a ranch with the killers the night before they ambushed Wellman. The morning of the murder, he saw three men steal out of camp: "Black Henry" Smith, Ed Starr and Charles Dembrey.

Sworn testimony from the coroner's inquest after Wellman's murder helps paint a clear picture of what happened next. The tracks of the three men showed that one of them stayed out of sight with the horses, while the other two hiked to the ambush site. Cigarette butts wrapped in yellow corn leaves, which were found at the site, verified the men had waited for Wellman.

One gunman crouched behind some sagebrush, while the other hid in a gulch about 65 feet from the left side of the rut road. When Wellman and Hathaway came in sight, they were caught in a crossfire. It took but one .44 caliber Winchester rifle shot—apparently from the man on the hill—to do the job. Wellman died quickly as the slug severed his spinal cord, ripped through his vital organs and lodged beneath the skin of his chest.

After the gang members made sure of their kill and removed the Colt from Wellman's holster, they fled, knowing full well they could never show off their loot.

So they buried it. And it may have stayed hidden forever, if not for Potts' discovery of the baking powder tin.

ONE FOR THE GRAVE

JOHN SHAW GIVES NEW MEANING TO BEING DEAD DRUNK

OUTLAW *John Shaw gulped his last whiskey while surrounded by five cowboys as the sun rose over the cemetery in Canyon Diablo, Arizona Territory. One problem: John Shaw was already dead.*

A DEAD GUY HAVING A PICK-ME-UP should fall squarely into the category of legend, and an easily dismissed one at that. But the story of Shaw's last drink is derived from photographs and eyewitness testimony. The episode exemplifies how the West was more than wild. Sometimes it was plain weird.

A GUNMAN'S OPERA

When Shaw and William Smith (a.k.a. William Evans) entered Winslow's Wigwam Saloon around 1:30 A.M. on April 8, 1905, they bellied to the bar and ordered drinks. But a stack of silver dollars on a nearby dice table proved more interesting. The two roughnecks drew pistols on the dice players and backed out the door with $271, never touching their drinks.

In their haste, the duo left a trail of coins near the railroad depot, leading lawmen to deduce that the thieves had walked the tracks before hopping a train. Navajo County Sheriff Chet Houck and Deputy Pete Pemberton tracked the outlaws to Canyon Diablo, 25 miles west of Winslow. They asked trading post operator Fred Volz if he'd seen the men. While Volz gave the officers a description of the men he'd seen, Smith and Shaw came into view, walking toward the depot.

Houck called, "I want to look you over."

The impetuous Shaw spun around and yelled, "You can't look me over!"

Shaw drew and fired from such close range, according to Flagstaff's *Coconino Sun*, that the powder burned Houck's hand. Luckily, the bullet passed through the sheriff's coat.

What followed was a kind of gunman's opera, mostly comedic, the players performing with jangled nerves under a cloud of hot smoke. Four men, as few as four feet apart, blasted at one another for the time it took to fire 21 shots. One man died. None of the others were badly hurt.

Houck killed Shaw with his final shot. The robber had run out of ammunition, and while Shaw was turned sideways, Houck fired a bullet through his head. Pemberton's last shot hit Smith's left shoulder as he zeroed in on Houck. The impact distorted Smith's aim, and the bullet nicked the sheriff's stomach, sparing his life. In addition to the fatal shot, the *Sun* reported that Shaw was hit in three places, and so was Smith, though not seriously.

A bullet also grazed Pemberton, who had violated a cardinal rule of gunmanship by putting bullets in all six chambers of his weapon, increasing the risk of an accidental discharge. (The other participants carried five bullets.) But Pemberton's boldness in loading that sixth round proved fateful. It decided the fight in favor of the lawmen and saved Houck's life.

"The death-fixed grin of a man who in life must've been easy going, happy-go-lucky."

Not content to let the deceased outlaw John Shaw rest in peace, a group of drunken cowboys opened his grave so he could meet his maker with a belly full of whiskey. Photos of the scene were captured for posterity. Here, two of the cowboys are caught propping up the dead bandit for his final drink.

"LET'S GIVE HIM A DRINK"

Volz provided a pine box from his trading post for Shaw's hastily-done burial, before the lawmen took Smith to the Winslow hospital. The next night, word of the shoot-out spread through the Wigwam Saloon, which was packed with cowboys from the Hashknife, a Northern Arizona cattle outfit.

Many of these cowboys had shady pasts that included rustling, and none liked the law. But what really got everyone hot was the idea that the robbers hadn't touched their drinks. Getting shot was one thing; being deprived of your paid-for whiskey was outrageous.

Fifteen of the cowboys got so worked up that they grabbed their whiskey bottles and jumped aboard the next train to Canyon Diablo. When they arrived, they pounded on Volz's door, waking him up.

Angry and aghast at their purpose, Volz eventually calmed down and loaned them shovels. He also gave the mob his Kodak square box-camera, saying Houck had wanted a photo in case of a reward.

"We stopped at the depot and had a few more drinks and then we went and dug the grave open with the shovels," a cowboy named Lucien Creswell said.

Cowboys stand around John Shaw's freshly opened grave after placing him back in his coffin with the whiskey bottle from which he had drunk his last sip—in death.

Shaw had a friendly grin on his face, "looking very natural, his head not busted open" by the bullet, Creswell added. "Some of the boys almost cried when they saw Shaw lying there so lifelike" but stiff as a board.

J.D. Rogers, the Hashknife's wagon boss, told the men, "Let's get him out. Let's give him a drink and put him away proper. Somebody can say a prayer, which wasn't done when they shoved him into that hole."

Two men dropped into the grave and "lifted the body upward into reaching hands," wrote Gladwell Richardson in *Arizona Highways* in 1963.

"They stood it up against the wood-picketed grave of another luckless man . . . and gave him a drink from a long-necked bottle, pouring the whiskey between the tight teeth, the death-fixed grin of a man who in life must've been easy going, happy-go-lucky," Richardson wrote.

As dawn broke, the cowboys jerked off their hats and mumbled a prayer. Into the casket they placed the bottle from which Shaw had drunk; then they returned the dead man to his rest.

PRISON MATES

The story of John Shaw's last drink also has a weird postscript.

Eight months after the gunfight, a drunken Pemberton, angry over gambling losses in Winslow's Parlor Saloon, shot town marshal Joe Giles five times, killing him. Pemberton was convicted of second-degree murder and sent to Yuma Prison, where William Smith was serving his sentence for the Wigwam robbery.

History doesn't record what prison yard chats the two must've had about their gunfight and its weird aftermath in the Canyon Diablo Cemetery.

EATING HIS WEIGHT IN DEMOCRATS

THE STRANGE TASTES OF ALFERD PACKER

IT was one of the most outrageous quotes of the Old West about one of the most barbaric crimes.

IN 1883, A 34-YEAR-OLD TRACKER NAMED ALFERD PACKER faced a judge and jury in Lake City, Colorado, as the only man in the United States ever charged with cannibalism.

At his sentencing, Judge Melville B. Gerry was said to declare: "Stand up, you voracious, man-eating son of a bitch, stand up! There was seven democrats in Hinsdale County and you up and ate five of them. God damn you, I sentence you to be hanged by the neck until you are dead, dead, dead, as a warning against reducing the democratic population of our state!"

Just reading the quote can transport you into a packed, crude courthouse in a backwater place; you can imagine the nodding heads and looks of satisfaction.

Too bad the quote is a fake.

TRACKING DOWN THE TRUTH

Yes, there really was an Alferd Packer (who is often called Alfred) and he really did kill five men and eat part of their bodies. And yes, there really was a Judge Gerry who sentenced him to hang. But the only part of that quote we are absolutely certain the judge uttered was, "until you are dead, dead, dead."

The clerk of the Hinsdale County Court tells *True West* magazine that the official entry in the record book includes those words, but otherwise, is a pretty straight-forward decree that Packer was to hang on the 19th day of May 1883.

But an old clipping from the *Rocky Mountain News* reported the judge had a lot more to say. The lengthy story appeared under a stack of headlines that included:

> *"THE HUMAN HYENA . . . Alfred Packer, the San Juan Man-Eater . . . After a Fair, Impartial and Honorable Trial . . . The Solemn Sentence Most Eloquently Pronounced."*

The newspaper quoted Judge Gerry as saying: "A jury of twelve honest citizens of the county have sat in judgment on your case, and upon their oaths they find you guilty of wilful and premedicated murder, a murder revolting in all its details.

"Stand up, you voracious, man-eating son of a bitch, stand up!"

BUILDING THE AMERICAN WEST

1883
The Union Pacific Railroad, directly and through partially-owned subsidiaries, controls 3,600 miles of rail tracks in the American West.

January 16
Pendleton Act is enacted, reforming civil service.

January 22
In Nevada, Wells Fargo messenger Aaron "Hold the Fort" Ross becomes a hero when he survives repeated attempts by five outlaws trying to get into the express car he is guarding.

Socialite Alva Vanderbilt.

February 5
The Southern Pacific Railroad completes its "Sunset Route" from New Orleans to San Francisco.

March 3
With its wooden ships, the nation ranks only 12th among naval powers, and so Congress authorizes construction of three metal cruisers for what will be known as the Steel Navy.

March 26
Alva, wife of railroad magnate William Vanderbilt, hosts what many believe to be the most lavish private party in American history at their home in New York City. Total bill: $250,000 (more than $3 million today).

May 1
Gen. George Crook crosses into Mexico in pursuit of Geronimo. Buffalo Bill Cody

Buffalo Bill Cody (center) and his acting troupe, which at one point included Wild Bill Hickok (second from the left).

"In 1874 you, in company with five companions, passed through the beautiful mountain valley where stands the town of Lake City. At that time the hand of man had not marred the beauties of nature—the picture was fresh from the hand of the Great Artist who created it. You and your companions camped at the base of a grand old mountain, in sight of the place where you now stand, on the banks of a stream as pure and beautiful as ever traced by the finger of God upon the bosom of earth.

He alone would walk out of the mountains.

"Your every surrounding was calculated to impress upon your heart and nature the omnipotence of Deity, and the helplessness of your own feeble life. In this goodly favored spot you conceived your murderous designs."

Judge Gerry went on for some time, admonishing Packer for his unimaginable crime.

GOLD-SEEKERS FIND BLOODY END

Packer had hired on as a guide for a group of 21 men from Provo, Utah, to Breckenridge, Colorado, in search of gold. Along the way, as things got rough, the group split, and Packer told the five men in his care that he knew a shortcut.

But there was no shortcut, and he alone would walk out of the mountains, fit and healthy—except for missing two front teeth—and claiming the five men had left him behind when he hurt his leg. He did look too healthy for someone who claimed to have survived as best he could, but it wasn't until he was seen carrying, not one, but two men's pocketbooks, that people really started getting suspicious.

Eventually, the townspeople found the camp below Lake San Cristobal where the bodies of the five men lay—four in a row, one a ways apart, all their skulls split open by a hatchet and one also shot in the back. And they found strips of human flesh.

Packer escaped before he could be brought to trial and wasn't found for nearly a decade. When he was captured, a jury convicted him, even though, to the very end, he proclaimed his innocence. It was late in the day when Judge Gerry finally sentenced him in a packed

stages his first "Wild West" show.

May 24
New York City opens the Brooklyn Bridge.

June 5
Wyatt Earp and Bat Masterson reach Dodge City, Kansas, to support Luke Short. While in town, they sit for their famous "Peace Commission" photo.

Frontier lawmen in the famed Dodge City "Peace Commission" photo.

August 1883
President Chester A. Arthur and other government dignitaries visit Yellowstone National Park. Arthur is the first president to visit the park.

November 3
The Supreme Court rules that Indians are "aliens" and dependents of the U.S. government.

November 17
Black Bart pleads guilty for robbing a stagecoach near San Andreas, California, and is sentenced to six years in prison.

November 18
The United States adopts the railroads' standardized time, henceforth dividing the nation into four time zones: Eastern, Central, Mountain and Pacific.

Stagecoach robber Black Bart.

December 8
Five so-called cowboys rob the Goldwater and Castenada Store in Bisbee, Arizona, and shoot up the town, killing four citizens in the process. It becomes known as the Bisbee Massacre.

courtroom where "a profound silence prevailed" so still that "the ticking of the clock was plainly heard," the *News* reported.

Judge Gerry, issuing the first death sentence ever imposed in Hinsdale County, declared that between the hours of 10 A.M. and 3 P.M. on May 19, 1883, Alferd Packer would be "hung by the neck until you are dead, dead, dead."

Alas, Packer did not swing until he was dead, dead, dead.

SOURCING THE QUOTE

So how did the judge's moving prose become the crude and outrageous quote that has so often been cited?

Tracing back through the quote's use over the years, in articles and books, it appears that it came from a barkeep and former acquaintance of Packer's named Larry Dolan. He told it to a reporter named Wilson Rockwell, who then printed it in *Sunset Slope.*

ESCAPING THE HANGMAN'S NOOSE

Alas, Packer did not swing until he was dead, dead, dead. He actually got a new trial. Since Hinsdale County did not exist when the crime was committed, it was deemed that authorities there had no right to put Packer on trial. The Colorado Supreme Court ruled on his appeal that the government couldn't hang a person for committing a crime before Colorado became a state. So he got a second trial, where the findings were the same, and he was finally sentenced to 40 years in prison.

In 1901, Packer was paroled by Gov. Charles Thomas. He lived out his life in Littleton, Colorado, where he died ten years later. (The town would gain notoriety for another heinous crime almost nine decades later, when two high school boys opened fire on their classmates at Columbine High School.)

Packer's name and legacy lives on. Phil Ochs memorialized him in "The Ballad of Alferd Packer," which goes: "Their guide was Alferd Packer, / And they trusted him too long, / For his character was weak, / And his appetite was strong."

In 1996, Trey Parker, of *South Park* fame, directed a raunchy spoof of Packer's story, *Cannibal! The Musical.* (In the credits, Parker uses the handle Juan Schwartz, similar to the alias John Schwartze, which was used by Packer while he was in hiding.)

The plateau above Lake San Cristobal has been christened Cannibal Plateau.

Even more telling is that students at the University of Colorado in Boulder named their cafeteria Alferd E. Packer Memorial Grill, and the university still holds an annual festival in Packer's name, which includes a raw meat-eating contest.

O HOMO

TOMBSTONE'S AU NATUREL VAGABOND

IN the summer of 1891, one of Tombstone's most infamous characters showed up in town without a gun, without a name and without clothes.

THAT'S RIGHT, WITHOUT CLOTHES. Except for a skull cap and crude leather sandals, this handsome, blue-eyed stranger—six feet tall, slightly bearded, of fine physique and intelligent bearing—was entirely naked. He also had a darn good tan.

The *Tombstone Daily Prospector* called him "the wild man of the weird and woolly west," and cracked that his attire "consisted principally of a lead pencil."

"I take pardonable pride in my cuteness," declared the bronzed visitor, who explained that a skin disorder prevented him from adopting the uncivilized convention of clothing.

That didn't cut it with Frank Broad, constable in the San Pedro River mill town of Charleston. With pistol drawn, Broad corralled his man, who promptly asked if newspapers had been writing about him.

"Yes," replied Broad, "they are full of it all over the East."

The prisoner puffed up and said, "I suppose you think you have made a big haul, but you will find yourself full for your pains."

Broad brought the naked man to Tombstone, nine miles distant, to stand trial for indecent exposure. His arrival touched off a sensational month of curiosity, speculation and uproarious philosophy from someone who refused to give his real name and insisted on being called O Homo.

"He has been traveling through the country stark naked," the *Prospector* reported on July 27, 1891, "and although he has frightened nearly everyone by his appearance . . . he talks perfectly rational and does not appear to be out of reason."

Far from it. O Homo was bright, well-read in Greek and Latin, able to quote Diogenes and other philosophers—and deeply thoughtful about baring every inch of his flesh.

Writing in the *Prospector*, which gave him almost unlimited space to air his views, O Homo penned, "The idea that poor women in New York chained to the treadmill of a labor-increasing machine, living on the crust of starvation, can make a better suit of clothing than God or nature . . . did God almighty make a mistake? . . . Zounds!"

In spite of his obvious love of nudity, O Homo was unwilling to give a straight answer to any personal question. When he stood before the judge to plead not guilty, he was asked his home state. "Do you expect me to testify against myself?" he responded.

Authorities had given him a straw hat, flannel shirt and blue overalls, which he wore under protest. He insisted on tossing a blanket over himself so that no sign of dreaded clothing was visible.

The *Prospector* declared him "the sensation of the year." Reporters dug for every morsel they could find about the cool and charming O Homo.

Following Tombstone's lead, other Western papers took up the story. A correspondent for the *San Francisco Chronicle* came to Tombstone to interview the prisoner, who'd speak

"He has been traveling through the country stark naked."

A rare look at the side yard of Fly's Photo Gallery and boarding house (above) where the "large magic lantern" image of O Homo was projected on the building to the left of the donkey (this is also the site of the so-called Gunfight at the O.K. Corral).

Another view (right), in 1905, from the courthouse looking north, shows Fly's property, which burned in 1912. Many priceless images, including perhaps photos and negatives of O Homo, were lost.

only after shedding his clothes. The *Chronicle* reported that O Homo was uncommonly good-looking, with the body of a prize fighter and "flesh hard as iron."

Speculation about him became a summer sport. One report said he'd been spotted walking west from Deming, New Mexico, along the railroad tracks "as naked as when born." He carried a canteen, a razor and a piece of white cloth, which he put on when approaching a town. Another said he'd walked up from Sonora, where Mexicans thought he was doing penance for his sins and advised him to pack a cross.

O Homo added to the circus atmosphere with various pronouncements, including that he was traveling the world on a $1 million bet. He also spent a good amount of time chastising Constable Broad. The prisoner revealed that he'd been arrested some 40 times prior to Broad getting hold of him. But he was never tossed in jail until he came to Tombstone—"and allowed myself to become a victim of fossilized ignorance in the form of a man who is not acquainted with a solitary water hole from the alpha to the omega of liberty."

Knowing it was sitting on a mountain of good copy, the *Prospector* shipped the prisoner a plug of chewing tobacco to keep him happy. The newspaper also published several of his teasing letters.

"Now, as I have excited a little curiosity in this quiet churchyard, I propose to offer this prize [a valuable jewel] to the man that ferrets out the mystery concerning me," wrote O Homo on July 29. He addressed his letter to the editor of the Daily Shoot Off, and signed it, "Yours Indecently."

On August 1, the *Prospector* published several guesses as to his identity, written by the jailhouse wag himself. They included the suggestions that he was Don Quixote looking for windmills and fair damsels and Oscar Wilde looking for sunflowers.

Was he also a presidential candidate? O Homo even suggested he was the "sockless statesman from Kansas making a sneak on the White House."

Readers sent letters to the editor positing their own theories. "Calls himself 'man,' but acts like a beast, entirely devoid of modesty," sniffed one. "Hence my reason for guessing him to be the missing link."

Another reader proclaimed him a tramp seeking notoriety and noted that she'd come to Arizona to hide away from the world, too. "With my clothes on," she emphasized.

O Homo was found guilty and sentenced to 30 days. He spent his time squatting on the floor, his shoulders covered with an oversized Indian blanket, or leaning in a picturesque pose against the wall of his cell. He had become so popular the *Prospector*, in effect, made him a columnist. His favorite topic was himself.

During his life in the wilds, O Homo said he had survived by eating a "palatable dish of

---

His writings alternated between insulting, rambling, hilarious and wise.

mud and water," mixed with mesquite leaves. He said the iron in the mud was the reason for his endurance, and he promised to perfect his dish and "make known to all mankind the process of its manufacture."

Among the Cheyenne tribe, O Homo was seen as the long-looked-for Indian Messiah predicted by Sitting Bull. Indians followed him in crowds, and he received the blessings of medicine men.

"They all displayed great anxiety to touch me," he wrote, "if only the hem of my blanket, and they offered me clothing which I firmly refused, telling them that it would be an insult to the great spirit to hide the form which he gave me from his sight by a bundle of the white man's rags."

When the Cheyenne asked O Homo to drive the evil from an insane man, he took a bottle of chloroform and poured some over his cap. He passed it under the man's nose, and "saying a few Latin words, I produced a profound slumber. He awoke with reason regained."

His writings alternated between insulting, rambling, hilarious and wise, such as when he remarked that he was the only man "in Tombstone who can truthfully say, I do not beg, steal, gamble or speculate."

Some samples of his writings . . .

On the sexes: "A man's honor and a woman's virtue are like a fort. No matter how strongly fortified, they can be taken."

On infamy: "I avoided settlements as much as possible for I was not seeking notoriety, but rather preferred to remain in the obscure corner of contentment, believing that the famous man is like a dog with a tin can tied to his tail."

On the *Prospector's* editor, who published one of O Homo's letters with a portion deleted: "I can overlook the drunken blunders of a tramp printer, especially when he is in the labyrinth of foreign words, but when an editor with ruthless negligence, strips the green leaves of wisdom, tramples upon the delicate flowers of pathos, and crushes the red-cheeked fruit of humor, and then with the stump whips his jaded horse to death, I feel like gently admonishing him to return to his old trade of butchering rotten carcasses and making sausage."

On happiness: "Reach to the most distant star and gather together the whole starry cosmos in your apron of wisdom, but know that all is but trash when compared to the brightest gem that ever adorned fair woman's brow, the only jewel worth wearing, the smile of contentment."

O Homo's writings attracted wide notice, and his fame grew. C.S. Fly, known for his photographs of Tombstone characters, began selling pictures of him. Even at the then-outrageous price of $1 apiece, they became a popular novelty.

Although none of Fly's photos of O Homo can now be found, there is no doubt the naked man existed. But his true identity was never determined.

After serving his time, the colorful stranger was released. He landed in Yuma in late October and "was decently dressed and conducted himself with propriety," according to the *Yuma Sentinel*.

He told the newspaper he was headed to Los Angeles to join a German professor on a trip "over the Colorado desert." After departing Yuma, O Homo vanished. (Or did he? See sidebar below.)

But he wasn't forgotten in Tombstone. For months afterward, drawn by flowery descriptions of his physique, women as far away as California wrote to O Homo, asking him to take a wife, namely the letter-writer.

If Wyatt Earp ever achieved that kind of adoration, the history books missed it.

Here's an artist's rendering of what the Fly photograph may look like.

O HOMO, WHERE ART THOU?

On Thursday, July 30, 1891, Camillus S. Fly offered O Homo $5 for a sitting at his Fremont Street photo gallery in Tombstone. Fly took three photographs that same afternoon.

On Sunday, August 1, the following article appeared in the *Tombstone Epitaph Weekly* about O Homo and the genius of C.S. Fly:

"A sheet stretched across the front of a vacant building next to C.S. Fly's Gallery, was made attractive last night by a life size transparency thrown upon it by a large magic lantern of O Homo. The crowds that visited this free show were greatly interested in Homo's history and discussed it without coming to any conclusion concerning his probable origin [or his] peculiar mode of travel."

Fly's photos of O Homo evidently sold well, for the *Prospector* reported, "Pictures of O Homo are in demand, and C.S. Fly is selling large numbers of them." One of the buyers was the *San Francisco Chronicle*, which published an engraving of the Tombstone celebrity (see image, p. 169).

On October 25, 1892, Tombstone newspapers reported that O Homo had committed suicide in Los Angeles, California. A suicide note was left behind.

—Gary S. McLelland

CHOMPIN' AT THE LIP

BILL PICKETT—BULLDOGGER EXTRAORDINAIRE

THE *world record for steer wrestling, or bulldogging, is 2.4 seconds (with barrier), which is roughly how long it takes to read this sentence.*

WITHIN THAT TIME, A COWBOY ON HORSEBACK has caught up with a running steer, weighing as much as 700 pounds, which is positioned between his horse and that of a hazer, whose job is to keep the steer running in a straight line. The cowboy slips off the right side of his saddle, locks his right arm in a half nelson around the right horn and grabs the left horn with his left hand. Digging his heels into the thick arena soil, while pushing down with his left hand and pulling against the horn snug in the crook of his right elbow, the cowboy brings the steer to a stop and throws it onto its side. Only after the steer's four legs are off the ground and pointed in the same direction does the clock stop.

Four men share this 2.4-second accomplishment, but the best time by the inventor of bulldogging isn't even close—eight seconds. He had a different technique, however. Bill Pickett wrestled steers to the ground using only his teeth.

ON HIS WAY TO FAME

Born 30 miles northwest of Austin, Texas, on December 5, 1870, Willie M. Pickett was the second child of 13 born to Thomas Jefferson Pickett and Mary Virginia Elizabeth Gilbert, the children of slaves. Willie was fascinated by the stories his male relatives told about cattle drives north to Kansas. In those days, it is estimated that one in six cowboys working in Texas was black.

By age 15, Willie became Bill as he grew toward manhood, working on various cattle ranches around Austin. He rode bucking horses on weekends for a little walking-around money, passing his dusty hat among the amused spectators.

He was 16 when he first threw a steer using only his teeth. Bill had seen bulldogs grab recalcitrant cattle by the snout and subdue them. If a bulldog could get those results, Bill figured he could, too. One day, he saw some cowboys having difficulty roping a herd of wild steers out of the thick brush that makes West Texas so special. He claimed aloud to the sweating cowboys that he could catch the steers and hold them with his teeth. The cowboys offered him the opportunity and Bill brought down three steers, one right after the other.

Word of Bill's feat got around and not long afterward, he accepted an invitation to travel to Nashville to perform his "bite 'em" style of bulldogging in a Wild West show.

Two years after his first appearance in a Wild West show, Bill moved with his parents to Taylor, Texas, and worked for a variety of cattle operations in the area. About that time, Bill met Maggie Turner. They were married in Taylor in December 1890, and they had nine children: two boys died before their first birthdays; all the daughters survived to adulthood.

He claimed aloud to the sweating cowboys that he could catch the steers and hold them with his teeth.

When a steer jumped the arena fence at Madison Square Garden in 1905, hazer Will Rogers turned the steer around, while Bill Pickett (above right) grabbed its head and wrestled it back to the arena.

Bill Pickett brings a steer down (left, top to bottom) by biting its lip in Cananea, Mexico, in 1906. If modern bulldoggers tried this stunt, they'd probably be classified insane.

Bill Pickett, the inventor of bulldogging, in action on the 101 Ranch, early 1900s.

EER. WITH HIS. TEETH. AT. 101 RANC

By 1900, Bill was performing bulldogging exhibitions as far west as Arizona and Colorado in partnership with different promoters. His reputation continued to grow, catching the attention of Zach Miller, co-owner of the 101 Ranch on the South Fork of the Arkansas River near Ponca City, Oklahoma. In March 1905, at an exhibition in Fort Worth, Texas, Zach convinced Bill to come work at his 101 Ranch and perform bulldogging as part of the Wild West show the Millers were building.

Bill moved his family to the ranch and found a cowboy's Shangri-la of lush pastures and open spaces. When he wasn't riding fence or herding cattle, Bill became part of the Miller Brothers' traveling show. He counted among his friends Will Rogers, Tom Mix and Hoot Gibson.

For a 1993 stamp series, artist Mark Hess painted Bill Pickett by using **The Bull-dogger** *poster (p. 175) as a reference.*

MATADOR CONTEMPT IN MEXICO CITY

Called the "Dusky Demon" throughout his career, to downplay his race, Bill was among the most popular performers in the show wherever it appeared, except Mexico City.

In December 1906, the Wild West show was having a difficult time drawing a crowd for its Mexico City performances. Bill was picking cotton back at the ranch when a telegram from Zach Miller's brother Joe requested that he come as soon as possible. Shortly after Bill's arrival, a group of matadors attended his performance. Their open contempt for it compelled Joe to propose a contest: Bill would bulldog any bull the matadors chose and prove his prowess with a fighting bull.

Bill had problems from the get-go. Fighting bulls, unlike steers, are thick at the shoulders and don't run away from the hazer. Bill managed to jump onto the bull after it gored his horse. The only secure hold he found placed him in front of the bull with his arms locked around the horns. Bill managed to hang on for almost eight minutes, until the crowd began throwing bottles into the arena. A bottle struck Bill and broke three of his ribs. He dropped free of the bull, but it took him a month to recover from the injury.

A 101 LIFER

Bill worked for the 101 as a performer and ranch hand for the rest of his life. The Great Depression killed the Wild West show and brought about the collapse of the 101 Ranch. On April 2, 1932, two weeks after his horse kicked him in the head, Bill Pickett died. Will Rogers announced Bill's passing on his radio show. In 1971, Bill Pickett became the first black cowboy inducted into the National Rodeo Cowboy Hall of Fame.

It's difficult to say which he enjoyed more, the spotlight in the arena or the sunlight on the range, but Bill Pickett loved the life he lived—the life of a cowboy.

VERA McGINNIS

THE MOST DARING COWGIRL WHO EVER RODE THE WEST

SHE *hardly even tried to describe the pain, but of course, how could she? What words are there to recount a ton of horseflesh landing on your tiny body, doing colossal damage: breaking your back in five places, busting three ribs, destroying a hip, shattering a collarbone, puncturing a lung?*

Vera riding Roman-style: standing on the backs of two galloping horses, she'd go around the ring to the cheers and yelps of an appreciative audience. She perfected tricks like this so quickly, many saw her as a natural horsewoman.

ON HER WAY TO BECOMING America's premiere woman rodeo champion, Vera McGinnis had been thrown before, stepped on before and dragged before, but even injuries permanent enough to require changes in her trick-riding act were nothing like this.

Years later when she wrote her autobiography, Vera devoted just a couple of pages to that day in 1934 when her trick pony Rosie somersaulted on top of her during a relay race. Nor does she dwell on the callous treatment she got in two hospitals—one pawning her off on the other, neither giving any medical care because she was poor, had no insurance and surely was dying anyway.

BUILDING THE AMERICAN WEST

1921
The Snyder Act grants responsibility for Indian social and medical services to the Department of the Interior.

Lindbergh's Spirit of St. Louis.

June 2, 1924
Congress passes a law making all of the nation's Indians citizens.

August 16, 1924
The last of the Bill Doolin Gang, Arkansas Tom, is shot dead.

July 21, 1925
John T. Scopes is found guilty of teaching evolution in Tennessee and is fined $100.

March 16, 1926
Dr. Robert H. Goddard launches the world's first successful liquid-fueled rocket, which travels 184 feet in 2.5 seconds.

May 21, 1927
Charles A. Lindbergh lands at Le Bourget airfield near Paris, France, having completed the first nonstop trans-Atlantic flight.

October 6, 1927
"Talking movies" arrive when *The Jazz Singer*, staring Al Jolson, opens in New York.

1928
U.S. Senator and Kaw Indian Charles Curtis is elected vice president under Herbert Hoover.

October 29, 1929
Stocks crash on Wall Street.

1930
Hoping the movie *The Big Trail* will make him a star, John Wayne sees his career plummet after the film fails at the box office. Smoot-Hawley Tariff is signed into law, helping to send the United States into a worldwide depression.

Many sold nickel apples during the Great Depression.

1931
Cimarron proves a box office success, winning an Oscar for best film. Wonder dog Rin Tin Tin makes his last movie, *Lightning Warrior*.

May 1, 1931
Empire State Building opens in New York City.

IT HAD TO BE IN HER GENES, or else how did Vera McGinnis do so many remarkable things:

♦ Jumped an irrigation canal on a "four-legged, crop-eared babysitting burro" named Croppie in 1895 when she was just three years old—a moment she recalled as "rodeo germ's first nudge."

♦ Won the very first riding competition she ever entered at age 13, taking home a gold-handled umbrella "which I needed like four legs."

♦ Learned to trick ride in just eight days in 1913 with such skill, on her first time out, she tied reigning trick-riding queen Tillie Baldwin.

♦ Ran the clock her first time on a bronc and her first time on a raging bull.

♦ Invented the "flying change"—getting from one horse to another without touching the ground—and was one of the few, man or woman, to circle a horse's belly at full gallop.

♦ Was the nation's only "girl jockey," competing and often winning in the "Sport of Kings" against the men.

♦ Won titles, trophies and prize money on three continents, appearing in more countries than any other cowgirl and earning the reputation as the girl who "rode the fastest and dared the most."

♦ Singlehandedly changed the fashion of the rodeo ring, as she was the first woman performer who dared to wear pants.

♦ Appeared as a Hollywood stunt double and was given a short film series until it became apparent her talent didn't match her beauty. (In *The Cimarron Land Rush*, she doubles for Estelle Taylor and is the only woman in the runaway scene, since all the others are men in wigs and dresses.)

♦ Wrote her autobiography, *Rodeo Road: My Life as a Pioneer Cowgirl,* published in 1974, which critics hailed as "one of the most authentic books ever published about the sport—a must-read for anyone interested in rodeo history."

♦ Inducted into the Cowgirl Hall of Fame in 1979 (and to this day, she's one of their favorite icons), and inducted into the National Cowboy and Western Heritage Museum's Rodeo Hall of Fame in 1985.

October 17, 1931
Chicago mobster Al Capone is convicted of tax evasion.

1932
Tom Mix makes his first talkie, *Destry Rides Again.*

March 9–June 16, 1933
Congress passes President Franklin D. Roosevelt's New Deal legislation to help stem the Great Depression.

December 5, 1933
Prohibition ends.

Cimarron was a box-office success.

1935
William Boyd makes *Hop-a-Long Cassidy*, the first film in this long-running Western series. Serial film *The Phantom Empire* establishes Gene Autry as the top singing cowboy in B-Westerns.

August 15, 1935
Cowboy comedian Will Rogers dies in an Alaskan plane crash.

1936
Boulder Dam (now Hoover Dam) begins operation. Margaret Mitchell's *Gone With the Wind* is published.

1939
Stagecoach boosts John Wayne's acting career, lifting it from the realm of the B-Western.

August 2, 1939
Albert Einstein sends a letter to President Roosevelt, warning him it's possible to make an atomic bomb.

October 23, 1939
Western novelist Zane Grey dies in Altadena, California.

September 14, 1940
United States begins its first peacetime draft.

The movie that made John Wayne a star.

You can't blame her. How could she bear to remember people who cared so little about a broken human being? But she does write how surprised she was when a doctor told her she probably wouldn't make it.

"I won't die," she told him.

"Then you'll end up a cripple," he said.

"No, I won't be that either."

She didn't die and didn't end up a cripple, but you have to imagine, at that moment, 42-year-old Vera McGinnis knew her days in the rodeo ring were over.

It had been a 21-year ride, and she'd forever have the gorgeous trophies won around the world and the mountain of newspaper clippings attesting to a prowess in the ring that made her "the girl to beat." But the year that should have been the pinnacle of her career, turned out to be the end. There's certainly no way to relate what that kind of hurt feels like. And so Vera McGinnis, one of America's pioneer cowgirls, kept it to herself.

Vera McGinnis began this incredible journey at a time when women didn't even wear pants around the house; when they wouldn't be seen in public without their corset; when they didn't have the right to vote and couldn't serve on juries. It was a time when professional opportunities for women were greatly limited: the few working outside the home made barely half as much as men. It was a time of strict codes and taboos, when women who displayed "masculine tastes"—such as competing in men's sports—were considered "sexual inverts."

And yet, Vera and her fellow buckaroos overcame all those restrictions and stereotypes to make their way in the rough and wild world of rodeos. As she began her career, over 200 women earned a living in rodeos or Wild West shows—about the best paying job open to women. Stars such as Mabel Strickland, Kitty Canutt, Prairie Rose Henderson, Fox Hastings, Tad Lucas, Ruth Roach and Florence Hughes Randolph left their mark forever. Vera McGinnis and these rodeo pioneers were America's first professional women athletes.

It had to be in Vera's genes, and it was. But not from her father as you'd expect—him being a dentist who encouraged his daughter's independence but preferred small towns to a ranch. No, the natural talent came from her mother Sarah, the real "ramrod" of the family and one of New Mexico's pioneer ranch women.

Vera's earliest memories were of the ranch her mother finally convinced her father to buy—a "cow outfit down on the Cimarron" near Clayton, New Mexico. The family moved to the ranch when Vera was three, but stayed only a few years, as the ranch never supported the family. By the time she was ten, the family had settled in a little town in Missouri.

So Vera wasn't raised as a ranch girl, like most who took to the rodeo circuit; she didn't even talk like a Western woman. Sure, she had an inkling for four-legged animals, but it was a two-legged, handsome cowboy who got her into the ring.

Her "undoing," as she'd later joke, came in the summer of 1913. Art Acord, a "big blond Don Juan" she'd met along the way, showed up in Salt Lake City for the Fourth of July's Frontier Day Celebration. Vera had recently moved to town to make her living as a stenographer. She passed for 18, but really was 21, and was pretty as a picture. (Today's popular actress Kristin Scott Thomas is her dead ringer look-alike.) Acord invited Vera out to the rodeo and gave her the lasting nickname of "Mac." She hung around to be near him, but Acord turned out to be a matchmaker, rather than a lover, and introduced her to the man who would steal, hold and then break her heart.

Vera at 18, already a beauty and already a girl who didn't fit the Victorian mold of the day. Although she wore her corset in her first relay race, that was a mistake she never made again, as she went on to change rodeo fashion forever.

Rodeo competitor Earl Simpson had sparkling black eyes, straight black hair, a cleft chin and was "a bit more reserved without a horse under him." Vera was instantly hooked.

Toward the end of the rodeo run, she overheard a promoter wishing he had another girl relay rider and she instantly volunteered. She took third. The next day she quit her job, packed her few belongings and joined the rodeo circuit.

"That was the decision that shifted the indicator on my life's chart," she'd write. "If I'd pulled up right then, I likely would have missed the years of hardship, heartache, fun, adventure, a smidgen of fame, and, finally, a broken body. But I'm glad I didn't, for I can honestly say the glamour never faded. It dimmed once in a while when I was hurt or overworked, but after a rest I always felt that I wouldn't trade being a rodeo cowgirl for any other profession."

She married Earl in 1914, but it would last only 10 often miserable years. Although she claimed he was her first husband, *True West* magazine discovered she had been married once before as a teenager, but that marriage lasted only a few months. In 1931, she would marry an "easy-going, big six-footer" named Homer Farra, who she stayed with until her death.

And who can decipher the real story of Vera's long relationship with the Sultan of Johore, one of the world's richest men? She met him on tour in Indonesia, and they communicated for decades afterwards—he sometimes signed his handwritten letters "please accept my little love to you." He shot tigers and panthers for her and sent the skins to her home in California. He also sent dozens of pictures of himself and was forever begging her for new snapshots. If she felt a "little love" for the man, she kept it to herself, although her scrapbook includes a clipping on his death in 1959.

No, love wasn't Vera's strong suit. But give her a horse, and she could do magic.

You've got to reek confidence to call yourself "The Greatest Show on Earth," but then nobody ever accused the Ringling Brothers of lacking moxie. When the Ringling Bros. and Barnum and Bailey Circus opened in New York's Madison Square Garden in March of 1923, it brought with it the reigning stars of the rodeo world and by now, Vera was one of them.

If the rodeo ring was dust and dirt, Madison Square Garden was spic and span. It all seemed so glamorous, especially the spectacular opening, when everyone rode through the ring in beautiful, if improbable, costumes.

"We rode black horses with gigantic hoopskirts hanging from our waists, the flounces reaching the ground," she remembered. Add to that the picture hats and ostrich plumbs, and you can see why she thought they "looked like mammoth Dresden dolls."

After the Garden, she joined the circus on its nationwide tour but soon jumped at the chance of giving Europe its first taste of a true rodeo. In 1924, Europe was a hoot for Vera McGinnis. She and nearly 200 of America's other top rodeo hands went over on an old troop ship with promoter Tex Austin for the "World Championship" at Wembley, England. "Without doubt, we were a thrilling sight to those Londoners who had never been any closer to our great West and its inhabitants than the motion-picture screen," she'd later write.

Vera got a humorous reminder she was on foreign soil when her landlady asked her "what time do you wish to be knocked up in the morning, Miss McGinnis?" Trying to keep a straight face, Vera said she'd like her wake-up call at seven A.M.

For the first performance, 93,000 people showed up and the rodeo stars became the toasts of London. Lavish dinners were thrown for them by the Prince of Wales, who hadn't yet met the woman he would abandon the throne to marry (and decades later, Vera's look-alike, Kristin Scott Thomas, would portray Wallis Simpson in the movies). London hostesses vied for the cowgirls and cowboys, requesting that they wear their Western clothes to the fancy parties.

The Wembley Rodeo was a 16-day show, with 32 performances. Vera rode one bucking horse a day, did a trick riding demonstration for the afternoon and evening shows, and rode a daily relay race. She won two world championships, the trick riding contest and the cowgirl's relay race. The rodeo was such a success, management decided to add another week. After that, another promoter booked Vera and other champions for a month at the London Coliseum, then the largest stage in the world. She later went to Dublin for that country's first rodeo. Vera would always keep a soft spot in her heart for Ireland, where she was treated like a movie star. When an injury demanded she spend a few days in bed, her room filled up with flowers from adoring fans.

She also won the trophy that would forever be

Earl Simpson and Vera on their wedding day in 1914: He was a handsome devil, great with horses, not so great at making a living or a home for a wife, and although she said it broke her heart when they split up, she did fine without him for decades after.

her favorite. It was made of elephant tusk with walrus-tusk handles. (Later, when she retired, she made it into a lamp and read by it in her favorite chair. The trophy has now been "delamped" and is on display at the Cowgirl Hall of Fame.)

By 1934, Vera McGinnis had seen the world, won about every rodeo championship, made enough to support herself—mostly just enough to get by—and was in excellent health for the first time in years. All the injuries she had suffered along the way were healed, and she was riding in fine form. Then came the relay race in Livermore, California, on June 10, 1934. "My big wreck," Vera would call it.

Reba Perry Blakely later wrote that she was riding beside Vera that Sunday. "Vera started whipping her relay mount and it fell—right in front of me but down on the rail, inside, and did a heels over head complete summersault, crushing Vera and her body into a railroad tie fence post. Horrible sound; a horrible sight for me to witness. Vera never again regained that wonderful, vivacious personality all we pioneers of rodeo knew."

"One minute I was a champion horsewoman, riding as well as I'd ever ridden in my life, the next, a crumpled heap," Vera stated in her autobiography.

But what happened next was even worse. "I was taken to a hospital in Livermore and X-rayed that afternoon. A nurse was kept busy removing the pan full of clotted blood that kept rolling out of my mouth. I couldn't speak; I couldn't even turn my head. . . . After visiting hours my doctor asked me about money. I made him understand there was no insurance or bank account for him to draw on, and the next thing I was aware of was being slid into an old rattletrap of an ambulance. This was seven hours later and still nothing had been done for me. Perhaps it was the money."

She was sent off to the Alameda County Hospital without anyone notifying her husband or the rodeo association, and without a shred of paperwork to explain who she was or what had happened. An angry attendant kept after her, and she finally struggled to explain she lived near Los Angeles. "No one wanted to touch me because I didn't live in Alameda County. Who had dumped me on them? It sounded as though they expected me to get up off that stretcher and leave!

"But dumped I had been and there I stayed until five o'clock the next afternoon without a single thing being done for me. Several times during that interval men in white came to my cot, lifted my right leg and rotated it in mid-air. I could hear the bones grind in my broken hip, and so could they, for they'd listen. I'd scream, of course, and the nurse would tell me to shut up. Then they'd lay the leg back down, not too gently and walk on. Once a different intern came on duty and when he read my chart he said, 'Is she still here?' It didn't occur to me that he thought I'd be dead by then."

Monday afternoon her husband finally found her and rushed her to Oakland Hospital, where she was told her chances of survival were slight. Five weeks later, she walked out of the hospital with the help of a cane.

A year later, Vera wrote to a friend in England, "I went to my first rodeo last Sunday at the Hoot Gibson ranch. Last year I won everything up there and this year I went as a Has Been. It has been a little hard to take but I have decided to sell my saddles and all my equipment. I

Vera and "The Girls" always got lots of attention when they performed at rodeos around the world, and it wasn't just because they were a pretty novelty: Vera was often lauded as an excellent horsewoman who could do almost anything on a horse, including besting men in relay races.

Vera's passport (inset) opened up a world few American women had a chance to explore, as it took her from one side of the globe to the other.

walk with a limp which I think I will overcome in time but I am going to try and get interested in something else."

Her new interest was writing her life story, which took her decades. The book was published in 1974 to glowing reviews, but poor sales. It is now out of print.

She and Homer settled into a quiet life in California. They raised thoroughbreds. Homer was a wrangler for the movies; Vera was devoted to her pets and her garden.

Vera remembered her first time on a bull in 1914: "The animal was so wide I felt as if I were straddling the dining-room table, and to top everything else, his hide was loose, and I rolled around like butter on a hot plate." But she ran the clock and was on her way to becoming "a real hand" in the rodeo world.

She had two last moments of fame as reporters again came calling to tell the story of a rodeo pioneer: in 1979, when she was inducted into the National Cowgirl Hall of Fame in Fort Worth, Texas, and then in 1985, when she was inducted into the Rodeo Hall of Fame in the National Cowboy and Western Heritage Museum in Oklahoma City.

"Many other aspiring cowgirls lacked her gritty resolve, and more than half the women who participated in professional rodeo during this era dropped out after only one or two years on the circuit," notes Mary Lou LeCompte in her book, *Cowgirls of the Rodeo*.

Eventually, Vera and Homer's health deteriorated so much, they were put in a nursing home in Northern California. Vera was confined to a wheelchair and outlived Homer. "Vera is very unhappy and is pretty much a problem as she has been so independent all her life," a friend noted.

Vera McGinnis Farra died on October 24, 1990. "She hadn't been in any pain," the friend reported. She was 98 years old, although her obituary stated she was 96 because Vera had shaved two years off her birth year.

"I would do it all over again," Vera said in one of her last interviews, "if they could leave out that last fall."

VERA'S PRESS CLIPPINGS

It's worn and tattered now, the black-bound "scrap book" she carried from one rodeo to the next. These are the press clippings and memorabilia of the 21-year career of Vera McGinnis, proof of how the world saw her.

It is a precious collection—no one could hope to reassemble these stories, printed on three continents from 1913–34.

It's easy to see her smiling as she clipped and taped another review, since this scrap book is populated with rave reviews—if she ever got "bad press," she didn't bother to keep it.

Looking every bit the beautiful movie star she tried to be, Vera poses in her California garden with some of her trophies, won on three continents. She had a tendency to make her favorite trophies into lamps.

Here's a sampling of newspaper clippings:

- **Sheridan, Wyoming, 1915:** Noting Vera is the nation's only "girl jockey": "The boy jockeys don't like to ride against a girl and they kick about it . . . but the spirit of American Fair Play in the audience always [prevails] and the girl is permitted to ride. As a usual thing, she wins. . . . Vera McGinnis is in a class by herself as an all- around cowgirl."
- **Prescott, Arizona, July 4, 1917:** "More rodeo prize money has been won by Vera McGinnis, fancy trick rider, than any other woman rodeo performer."
- **Phoenix, Arizona, November 14, 1917:** "On a high spirited, flea-bitten gray, Vera McGinnis, claimant to the world championship among women vaqueros, led off the cowboy sports program with a drunken cowboy act that startled the spectators. Quaffing nothing stronger than soda pop from a flask, Miss McGinnis stood on her horse's withers with the animal in a dead run and reeled backward and forward and sidewise until it appeared as though she would topple from her unstable mount into the dust track. But not so. The daring girl piloted her steed several hundred yards and brought him to a halt without losing control for a moment."
- **Headline in London, 1925:** "The Most Discussed Women in Town, Rodeo Cowgirls," pictures Vera with her peers.
- **Indonesia, 1926:** "Miss Vera McGinnis, the acknowledged champion girl rider of the world, who won two championships at Wembley last year and well over 100 other cups and medals in all parts of the world, gave a thrilling exhibition of trick riding."
- **Colorado Springs, Colorado, 1926:** Vera "can do anything on a horse" and is "about the finest horsewoman in the game."
- **Hanford, California, (no date, probably 1933):** Announcing Vera was a "special attraction" at the Pioneer Day Celebration: "for six years world's champion trick rider among women and holder of records all over the world . . . called the best dressed cowgirl ever appearing in Madison Square Garden, Miss McGinnis also has a nationwide reputation as a bronc and steer rider, often competing with the best of the men riders. Miss McGinnis carried off all honors at the 1932 California Rodeo."
- **Livermore, California, June 15, 1934:** Reporting her "precarious" condition after Sunday's bad accident, adding: "Miss McGinnis . . . is extremely popular here, having been a regular performer for the past 15 years. She had appeared at every show of consequence in this country and in Europe."